WHAT PEOPLE ARE SAYING ABOUT
Trapped in the Magic Mirror

From the moment you pick up this book you will recognize the truth in its pages. Trapped in the Magic Mirror *replaces fantasies with facts and provides the reader with a realistic plan for creating happily ever after. A must-read for the relationship savvy!*

—PAT LOVE, ED.D.
AUTHOR OF *THE TRUTH ABOUT LOVE*

What an important message! Every mom will want to read this book and then teach these valuable insights to her daughter. Deborah communicates truth that will transform the way you think about yourself, about marriage, and about the beauty that God has given you. It's a book to read over and over again.

—DR. SCOTT TURANSKY
COFOUNDER, NATIONAL CENTER FOR BIBLICAL PARENTING, AND
AUTHOR OF *PARENTING IS HEART WORK*

Trapped in the Magic Mirror, *by Deborah Dunn, holds out real help to every Christian wife who may feel that her marriage lacks the sparkle, romance, and intimate friendship that she longs for. Using the "magic mirror" as a metaphor for the illusion we harbor in our hearts of how life "should be," Dunn leads the reader to recognize her "magical thinking" about marriage. From that point, she is able to help the reader make changes in the way she relates to her husband. Dunn is a great communicator—witty, intelligent, and willing to reveal her own past weaknesses in order to lead her reader to a place of new strength.*

—CLAIRE CLONINGER
AUTHOR OF *101 MOST POWERFUL PRAYERS IN THE BIBLE,*
LETTER FROM HEAVEN, AND THE *E-MAIL FROM GOD* SERIES

To read Trapped in the Magic Mirror *is to take a journey through a woman's soul. This book will teach you how to free yourself from the illusion in the mirror and become your authentic self. Ms. Dunn gives practical advice and an inventory to assure characterization of self using God's definition and not the world's. That freedom is essential to creating harmony in friendships and marriage. This is a must-read for any woman struggling with who God wants her to be and who the world says she is.*

—ERIC AND JENNIFER GARCIA
COFOUNDERS, ASSOCIATION OF MARRIAGE & FAMILY MINISTRIES

DEBORAH B. DUNN

TRAPPED in the MAGIC MIRROR

SHATTERING ILLUSIONS *about* ROMANCE *and* MARRIAGE

LIFE JOURNEY®

Bringing Home the Message for Life

COOK COMMUNICATIONS MINISTRIES
Colorado Springs, Colorado • Paris, Ontario
KINGSWAY COMMUNICATIONS LTD
Eastbourne, England

Life Journey® is an imprint of
Cook Communications Ministries, Colorado Springs, CO 80918
Cook Communications, Paris, Ontario
Kingsway Communications, Eastbourne, England

TRAPPED IN THE MAGIC MIRROR
© 2006 by Deborah B. Dunn

The Web addresses (URLs) recommended throughout this book are
solely offered as a resource to the reader. The citation of these Web sites
does not in any way imply an endorsement on the part of the author or
the publisher, nor does the author or publisher vouch for their content
for the life of this book.

Cover Design: Zoë Tennesen Design
Cover Photo Credit: Mirror: Ryan McVay/Photodisc
                     Stars: Photodisc

First Printing, 2006
Printed in the United States of America

1 2 3 4 5 6 7 8 9 10 Printing/Year 11 10 09 08 07 06

ISBN: 0-7814-4284-2

LCCN: 2005937735

*To all the precious women
whom I have counseled through the years,
who are struggling to look beyond the flaws they
see magnified in their mirrors to the beautiful
women God truly intended them to be.*

*To my nephew, Jody West,
and his mom, Patti West,
you have a special place in my heart.*

CONTENTS

Part 3: Shattering the Mirror

ACKNOWLEDGMENTS

When any Christian gets to the point where she can actually write a book, she's usually been through a lot of valleys, and those valleys can be pretty dark and lonely at times.

I can say without any reservation that the people I wish to name here have seen me through many of those valleys when I couldn't even think or pray, much less write. Their belief in me often surpassed my belief in myself. I cannot adequately thank them for their love and friendship, and I hope we continue to walk along the same path for the remainder of our lives.

If I have failed to mention someone important, please forgive me.

To the friends who know me, warts and all, and love me anyway: Sherie Lewis, Susan Thompson, Becky Mitchell, Carol Pullen, Cindy Morris (aka Roxanne), Patricia Bowen, Melody McKay, and all the old friends who've stuck with me through the years. I love you all dearly, and I am so grateful God gave you to me as the girlfriends every woman has to have to make it through life without going under.

To the editors, writing partners, and mentors who gave me encouragement and treated me like a professional even before I was one: Melissa Slagle, John Birch, Marlene Bagnull, Peggy Payne, Pamela Duncan, Lee Smith, and a special thanks to my dear and very kind editor, Mary McNeil, at Cook Communications and her very tactful and diplomatic assistant, Diane Gardner, whose diligence and patience are worthy of a crown. I am so honored to be a part of the Cook team. Then there is the ubiquitous Jeff Dunn, editor of the RiverOak division, who first had the idea that this book should be written and though we are not related at all, immediately made me feel as if I were part of his long lost tribe of distant cousins.

To my fellow colleagues and counselors: my old Methodist Home and Crossnore School buddies, all the social workers and therapists who worked with me in the trenches and blessed me by purchasing my first self-published book, and my wonderful clinical supervisors through the years—you have taught me how to make therapy an art form which flows like a river of creative expression and inspiration in my life. Many thanks to my publicist Tom Wright, and to my friend H. Norm Wright.

I wish to thank the Carolina ChristCare team: John Mark Batchelor, Debbie Hilliard, Diane and Cliff Bean, Jim Babson, Larry Iuso, Kristen Cowan, Machelle Bass, Tamla Boone, Shannon Manning, Chris Dyer, and Jan Hamburg. You have caught the vision for teaching churches how to respond to disaster and your dedication to our cause thrills me.

To the spiritual warriors who helped pray me through the completion of this book: the prayer team at White Oak Baptist Church, Robert and Josie Kornegay, John and Carol Pullen, Donnie Cook, Bill Edwards, Ruth Linebrink, and any others who have prayed for me through the years.

I thank my very kind and patient husband, Rick Dunn, for his love, faithfulness, and honesty. I thank my son, Lee Dunn, for not only being a wonderful son, but a good friend as well. I thank my beautiful and talented daughter, Greyson Dunn Briere, for teaching me so much about life. My gratitude goes to my mom and dad for never losing faith in my ability to pull this off! Thanks to my sisters, Beth Wilson and Teri Matheson, and their husbands, for sharing this life journey with love. And God bless my nephew, Nick, and nieces, Brooke and Erin, for giving me hope that there is still a bright future for the world as long as children as beautiful and loving as they are still in it.

Deepest thanks to Grandma Birdie Dunn, whose excitement about this book was such a joy to me. Sincere gratitude to David and Julia Dunn and the boys for being such a fine example of a Christian family. And heartfelt appreciation to Shirley Dunn, whose life has been a gift to all of us, as she has shown me how important it is to endure difficulty with grace and long-suffering, without losing faith in God.

May he richly bless you all!

FOREWORD

BY DR. NORM WRIGHT

The title of this book is enough to pique anyone's curiosity and draw them to this resource of substance. But why would a man write a foreword to a book that is primarily for a female audience? Perhaps it's because I've counseled hundreds of women as well as written two books, which hopefully spoke to the issues they face (*Always Daddy's Girl* and *A Dad Shaped Hole in My Heart*).

I'm delighted to have the privilege of discovering a very practical book that speaks clearly and directly to four issues that impact the journey of many women. Over the years I've read numerous books that contain helpful content but have left much to desire in their presentation. That is *not* the case with this one, for it reaches out to draw you into its message. It is not a book of fluff, but of substance. Many of the readers will wonder, *Were you reading my diary? You're talking about my thoughts and feelings.* That is what you can expect if you peruse the pages.

You will discover that Deborah will bring you back to reality, but in a gentle way so that you will be encouraged rather than despairing. I particularly like the writing style, which mixes stories with solid information and even includes sections stating "Here's what you can do next...." The author uses personal examples, but they aren't overdone and show you that she has "been there." The scriptural teaching fits well and is an integral part of the message rather than simply being tacked on to make it sound "Christian."

If you connect with this, you're in for a journey of learning and change. When you've finished reading this book, I'm sure that you will want to pass it on to others for them to hear the message.

Dr. Norm Wright

INTRODUCTION

The power of a good story fascinates me. A story can work its way into our hearts and change our lives in profound ways even while we are simply having fun. Jesus—the master storyteller—knew well the power of stories to reach us on a very deep level.

For a number of years, I've used writing of all kinds in my therapy practice. Journaling, storytelling, poetry, and letters are all powerful ways to aid the healing process. In fact, I started writing years ago because of my own grief and depression, never realizing God would one day lead me to write a book to help bring women out of the very darkness I experienced myself.

Like parables, fairy tales have an uncanny ability to illustrate values and beliefs and to mold how we think. That power is not always a good thing, especially if the fairy tales send false messages. Unfortunately, many do just that.

Occasionally, I try my hand at writing a fairy tale that sends good messages. One of my favorites is the story of Isolde, a beautiful but unhappy princess who suffers a long and difficult journey in order to find her true self and feel beautiful in God's eyes.

THE MIRROR WAS

ACTUALLY PART OF

HIS EVIL PLAN.

Isolde's father is a kind and gentle king in a land called Far Away. Her mother had died giving birth to her. Isolde is their first and, therefore, their only child. Motherless, lonely, and isolated from the world outside, Isolde grows to be a very insecure young woman, dependent upon her father's constant attention and affection.

On her sixteenth birthday, her father gives her a huge party and invites all the other members of court and their families to the big event. They each present Isolde with a gift fit for a princess. But one of the lords in attendance is very evil and wants to overthrow the kingdom. He presents Isolde with a Magic Mirror and tells her it will make all of her wishes come true.

But the mirror is actually part of his evil plan. He had sought the aid of witches, who cast a spell on an ordinary mirror so that it would tell the princess lies—lies that would prey on her loneliness and insecurities and lead her to make terrible life choices. The witches knew Isolde's mistakes would eventually cause her so much emotional pain that she would sicken and die, the king's heart would break, and the kingdom would be destroyed.

That is exactly what happens. Isolde begins to rebel against her father. Her rebellion leads her into painful relationships and shameful behavior. Finally, alone in the Dark Forest and nearing death, the princess realizes that the mirror is killing her.

Summoning her last ounce of strength, she smashes it against a rock. As the broken glass falls to the ground, the shards turn into drops of healing water, which collect in the cleft of a rock. The good king finds his tattered and ragged daughter near the pool of healing water and rescues her by using the water to cleanse her wounds until she is healed. She drinks the remainder of the water and becomes well and strong. The bedraggled princess takes her rightful place alongside her father and the kingdom is saved.

But like so many of my early stories and poems, the story of Isolde and her Magic Mirror languished in my filing cabinet, forgotten for many years.

If you want to know the truth, I had never given much thought as to how the idea for this book was born until one of my editors specifically asked the question. I realized I didn't really know—it just always seemed to have been there. It wasn't until I needed to write this

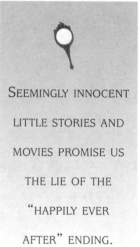

SEEMINGLY INNOCENT

LITTLE STORIES AND

MOVIES PROMISE US

THE LIE OF THE

"HAPPILY EVER

AFTER" ENDING.

introduction that the Lord reminded me of Isolde, and I can tell you that was a moment of pure joy. I felt like a gardener who planted a precious seed, forgotten it for many years, and then walked out in the garden one day to see an entire tree growing!

Now the seed has come to fruition, and this is certainly no longer a child's simple story. I thank God for inspiring the story and for his faithfulness in bringing it forth in this book.

The Magic Mirror is a symbol I've borrowed from fairy tales I've used to describe how our thoughts become distorted when we seek affirmation from sources other than God. The process starts when we are small children, especially those of us exposed a great deal to fantasy and fairy tales. Seemingly innocent little stories and movies promise us the lie of the "happily ever after" ending, where the prince always rescues the princess, and they never suffer any hardship or pain.

As we grow up, we continue to devour movies, television, magazines, and books that promise more of the same, except the romance becomes more intense and the marketing more suggestive. We become obsessed with our weight, clothes, homes, credentials, and bank accounts. We fall prey to illusions that life will be wonderful if we become the perfect woman. We will find "Mr. Perfect" and he will adore us. Then we get married and can't understand why our real lives and marriages aren't what we imagined.

WE FALL IN LOVE WITH THE IMAGINARY MAN WE THINK WILL GIVE US THAT GUARANTEED HAPPY ENDING.

But in spite of our sometimes rude awakenings, we still cling stubbornly to our romantic illusions. We do not realize we have become addicted to them. The problem is that those illusions are so much more fun than reality!

Yet that is exactly when they become the most destructive and dangerous. Romance may be the balm that soothes our wounded souls, but after a while an obsession with romance becomes a weapon that breaks our hearts, ruins our marriages, and ultimately destroys our spirits.

Before we know it, we are seduced into painful sexual experiences, abortions, divorces, and eventually the breakdown of our families—all in the name of love and romance. Christian families are not immune. Many have been destroyed by those lies.

Unfortunately, addiction to romance and "romantic thinking" has become quite socially acceptable. Romantic thinking is the term I use to define thought processes that allow us to see what we want to see instead of what is really true. In most circles these days, romance is thought to be quite innocent and harmless. Yet the Bible is full of admonitions about the pitfalls of romantic thinking. Just read the book of Proverbs!

I'd like to be able to say that my training as a therapist has taught me all this, but the truth is that most of what I have learned through the years has come the hard way. I also learned a lot from reading wonderful books by Dr. Pat Love, Dr. Harville Hendrix, Melody Beattie, Gary Smalley, and many other authorities in their fields, most of whom I've included in the resource section at the end of the book. I've had incredible clinical supervisors and seminar teachers throughout the years as well. The rest I've gleaned from counseling hundreds of women over the past twenty years.

I've personally had to *unlearn* a great deal along the way as well, and sometimes the lessons were quite painful. But in spite of a somewhat bumpy ride on this life journey, I am thankful to my very patient and loving husband, Rick, who has been a rock throughout my learning process and the thirty-seven years of our marriage. We both realize marriages lasting as long as ours has are getting rare these days. We chuckle with each other when people look at the two of us as if we need to be placed in a museum somewhere, along with the rest of the dinosaurs.

With a divorce rate of well over 50 percent now, it is very common for many adults to be married two or three times in their lives. There are research studies suggesting that the divorce rate is even higher among Christians, especially those who claim to be "born-again" (Barna Research Group, www.barna.org, December 21, 1999).

Since I consider myself to be in that subcategory—along with many of the women I counsel—this is disturbing to me. But truthfully, I am not surprised. Ironically, I think the very part of our personalities that may predispose us to an attraction to religion and mysticism may also be a hindrance to our exercise of logic and rational thinking if we are not spiritually mature. Our ability to exercise a strong faith in the unseen— a gift from God and a wonderful strength—can be the very part of our selves that expects too much of our lives and relationships, particularly our marriages. Sometimes there is a very thin line between faith and denial. When we cross that line, we can fall prey to expecting the miracle of the happy ending, no matter how many obstacles are in our paths, how flawed our logic, or how little positive action we choose to take to make our dreams come true. At the first sign of trouble, when we feel cheated of that miracle ending, we become angry and discouraged. We forget that in order to love like God loves us, we have to have patience and long-suffering. But instead of waiting on God and loving our man like he is, we fall in love with the imaginary man we think will give us that guaranteed happy ending.

The truth is that at least every other couple I counsel these days comes to my office because the woman has "fallen out of love" with her husband, or she does not believe that he is showing her the kind of love that she feels she needs. Thinking her life was going to be so much more exciting and romantic than it is, she has become disappointed, angry, and frustrated because she believes she is being taken for granted. She no longer enjoys sex, she has become depressed, and she feels emotionally disconnected from her husband.

In many cases, she truly is being taken for granted. But often her husband's lack of attention stems from his own anger and frustration because her demands seem overwhelming.

Nothing he does is right and no matter what he does he feels he cannot please her. So after a while he just quits trying at all. They become "stuck" in a destructive cycle of accusation, blame, and bickering.

In a larger sense, women prone to fall into the "trap" of romantic thinking are also the ones who never seem to feel good about their lives on any level. No matter how much money they make, weight they lose, or how good they look, nothing is ever enough. They are angry and dissatisfied. They feel something is missing.

OUR ULTIMATE GOAL IN LIFE SHOULD BE TO LOVE GOD WITH ALL OUR HEARTS, MINDS, AND SOULS.

The trap door widens when she begins to compare her husband with other men. When he comes up short, she makes the mistake of trying to "improve" him. She may drag him to a marriage retreat or Bible study, hoping he will take the hint that he needs to change.

He might, at his wife's urging, even go as far as attending a Promise Keepers Conference or joining a men's group in church. But after a few months, the promises are forgotten. The marriage falls right back into the same cycle. She begs for more romance and attention. He shuts her off and tunes her out. She becomes sarcastic and critical. He digs his heels in deeper.

Disappointed and angry, she turns to her Magic Mirror of romantic thinking. The mirror tells her to work harder on her external attributes and become a better wife, with the promise that if she does so her husband will reciprocate by changing himself into the man of her dreams—the man the mirror tells her she really needs.

She tries. But when the results don't materialize, the mirror tells her she shouldn't have to live like this. Just like the serpent and Eve, the mirror tells her she doesn't have to listen to God. Suddenly it seems as if divorce and remarriage could be the answer to all her problems, especially when someone who makes her feel beautiful and special happens to cross her path.

WE'RE OFTEN DISSATISFIED WITH OUR HUSBANDS BECAUSE WE'RE DISSATISFIED WITH OURSELVES.

Trust me, our Adversary will always send that someone just when marriages are the most vulnerable.

The effect of infidelity and divorce is particularly devastating in Christian marriages and has the potential to spiritually cripple a woman for life. Children suffer in the aftermath, not only because of the resulting broken home, but because parents are often more focused on their own romantic entanglements than on parenting their children.

But it is not just families who are suffering—our churches suffer as well. The church is a body, and when one part of the body is in pain, it reverberates throughout the whole body. And much of it begins with the very simple craving human beings have for romance, escape from reality, and the fairy-tale life.

Unfortunately, without realizing it, some churches actually encourage women to indulge in romantic thinking and escapism. More emphasis is placed on entertainment, food, social interaction, and event planning than on spiritual growth and renewal. Christian romantic fiction sales are at an all-time high. The subtle inference is that our primary role as a Christian woman is to find the perfect husband, make him happy, have children, and serve on committees in church. If we do that we will experience wonderful romance and happiness. If that doesn't happen, it is inferred we must be doing something terribly wrong.

But the Bible says our ultimate goal in life should be to love God with all our hearts, minds, and souls. It doesn't say a thing about landing the perfect mate, nor does it indicate that real love and marriage depend at all on romance, at least not over the long haul. And the Bible talks a lot about suffering and hardship.

I'm not trying to say that all the problems in marriage come from addiction to romance or that the woman who enjoys a light romance novel or movie every now and then is a romance addict. It is not wrong to want a better marriage or to want your man to love and serve God and to treat you well. We should expect warmth, intimacy, and affection in our marriages no matter how long we have been married. God wants peace in our marriages.

But I believe we're often dissatisfied with our husbands because we're dissatisfied with ourselves. We yearn for what we don't have, and we fear that we are missing out on our "soul mate." We've been brainwashed by media and marketing into believing that nothing we do or have is good enough. We've been bombarded by continual messages all our lives that there's an illusive *something more* out there that will make us happy. When we don't find it, disillusionment and discouragement become our daily battle.

If you feel this way, you are not alone or different from other women. We have all been brainwashed to some degree or other, and many of us are trapped in a magic mirror. Nearly all of us carry emotional baggage. But if we are going to be satisfied with our lives and happy in our marriages, we have to learn how to leave behind the myths we believed as children—the myths that are distorting our thinking as women today.

I want to help you let go of those destructive myths so that you can finally experience contentment and peace in your life. It took me a long time to find it in my own life, and I don't want your struggle to be as difficult as mine was.

You may not think this book applies to you. Only you know for sure. However, I think a lot of women do not talk about their feelings for fear of being thought silly or "not spiritual enough." My experience is that many women suffer in silence, pretending to be happy with their lives, constantly worrying about whether they "measure up" to other women, and wondering why they haven't been invited to that big party they're certain is going on somewhere.

I realize your marital problems may be more complicated and difficult than what I've described here. You may need a great deal more help than this book can give you. It's possible you're married to someone who treats you terribly. I deal with those tougher problems in my practice every day. Substance abuse, physical violence, verbal abuse, pornography, and perversion are very destructive and lead to grave consequences if they are not treated as the serious problems they truly are. There have been many excellent books written about these problems and there are many good Christian therapists.

Likewise, I am not asking you to submit to a spouse who is not a good man. Nor do I want you to pretend that your husband is wonderful when he is not. I am *not* asking you to indulge in denial. I *am* asking you to accept the fact that you cannot change your husband. If you want peace, *you must focus on changing yourself.*

I realize that many of you out there are reasonably happy, so you may think this book does not apply to you. Perhaps you just want a better marriage, or you counsel others. Some of you have overcome great obstacles already. You could be one of those women whose marriage hasn't really been tested yet. Perhaps there has been no huge crisis that has really challenged your faith or your marriage.

Maybe you think I'm just being silly. Maybe you think there can never be too much romance and I'm only trying to spoil your fun.

Be careful you don't stare too long into that mirror. Trust me, it will lead you down a path to deep woods and dark places.

PART ONE

STEPPING INTO THE MIRROR

CHAPTER ONE

LIFE IN THE MAGIC KINGDOM

*Jesus answered and said to her, "Whoever drinks of this
water will thirst again, but whoever drinks of the water
that I shall give him will never thirst."*

—John 4:13–14

When I was a little girl about the age of six or seven, I
absolutely loved Sundays. Not only did I get to see all my
friends at Sunday school and sing about Jesus having the whole
world in his hands, but I got to color pictures while listening to
amazing stories—*true* stories, we were reminded—from the
Bible. We heard about how the baby Moses was rescued from
the bulrushes to grow up to be a prince, and about Jonah, who
escaped the belly of a "great fish." We were horrified when Eve
ate the forbidden fruit, and we thrilled to imagine Jesus one day
returning on a white horse to save us.

After church, we'd often go to my grandma's house for a lunch of fried chicken and homemade biscuits. Afterward, I'd get to play in the attic all afternoon with my cousin Becky. The game we loved to play the most was "dress up." Grandma High would give us old white bed sheets, costume jewelry that we pretended were diamonds, a broken tube of "Cherries in the Snow" lipstick, and a couple of pairs of rundown high heel shoes.

WE TOOK FOR GRANTED THAT A WEDDING WAS SUPPOSED TO LEAD TO SOMETHING WONDERFUL AND PERMANENT.

First, we'd wrap the sheets around ourselves like a Greek tunic and pin them at the shoulders with safety pins. Then we'd take turns doing the other's hair up in a French twist and painting our lips bright red. After hours of preparation, we'd stand in front of the full-length mirror in the bedroom, staring at ourselves and fantasizing about our bright, beautiful futures.

Becky was tall, lean, and willowy, but I was rather short for my age and a bit chubby. Wobbling on our high heels and pretending to smoke cigarettes like the movie stars did, I'm sure we were quite the comical pair. But we thought we were the epitome of glamour and sophistication, especially when we'd pretend that our boyfriends were coming any minute to pick us up for the prom or, best of all, that we were brides about to be married. Fresh gardenias and hydrangeas made beautiful bridal bouquets or corsages, and we'd take turns humming "Here Comes the Bride" as we marched down the aisle.

From the age of five, when her mother died of kidney disease, Becky lived with our grandparents. Our grandfather was a weekend alcoholic, but no one ever really talked to us about it except to warn us to keep our distance when he was drinking. Though he never hurt any of us, we surely didn't want to find out what would happen if we pushed him too far. We just pretended everything was fine. Unfortunately, we learned how to pretend far to well.

A lot of pretending went on back when I was young. People didn't talk a lot about their problems. After all, what would the neighbors think? Even though Becky and I sensed that a lot of grown-ups we knew didn't seem happy, we never realized that had anything to do with marriage. In fact, we never really thought about marriage much at all, except for the part where you got to be a beautiful bride and "live happily ever after," whatever that meant. All we knew was what we saw on television and in the movies, where every girl dreamed about her wedding to a handsome man. We took for granted that a wedding was supposed to lead to something wonderful and permanent, especially if there was a lot of romance in the meantime. No one ever talked to us about what happened when the honeymoon was over!

As much as I enjoyed Sunday school and going to Grandma's, the best part of Sundays happened later at night, back home, when it finally came time to watch my very favorite television program, *Disneyland* (known to later audiences as *The Wonderful World of Disney*).

Fresh from my bath, I'd curl up on the couch, nibble on a cookie, and stare wide-eyed at the old black-and-white television casting flickers of light out into the dark pine-paneled den. After all these years, I still remember how I tingled in anticipation, waiting for that familiar music to swell to its wonderful crescendo, filling my heart with endless possibilities for the future. The syrupy chorus seemed to promise a life full of adventure, beauty, romance, and magic.

When you wish upon a star ...

You know the rest.

Tinkerbell arrived out of nowhere and dipped and swirled across the screen. With one flick of her wand, that ethereal little imp with her glittering fairy dust would bid the gates of the kingdom to swing wide open, beckoning all little children everywhere to enter in. It didn't matter if you were poor or plain or if you had an unhappy family. You were always welcome in Disneyland: the Magic Kingdom.

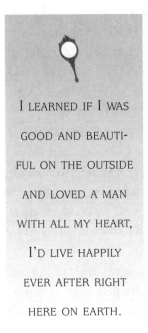

I LEARNED IF I WAS GOOD AND BEAUTIFUL ON THE OUTSIDE AND LOVED A MAN WITH ALL MY HEART, I'D LIVE HAPPILY EVER AFTER RIGHT HERE ON EARTH.

Growing Up in the Magic Kingdom

And enter we did—by the millions. Every Sunday night for over half a century, little girls all over the world waited in awestruck wonder for the gates of that fantasyland to open and let them in. For it was there that they could forget their ordinary lives for an hour and be transported to a place where there was always a happy ending.

In the Magic Kingdom, terrible beasts turned into wonderful husbands. In that glorious place, rather ordinary girls turned into royalty, and the prince never failed to show up on time. Best of all, if she was pretty and sweet enough, he'd sweep the girl off to a problem-free life—a life without illness, mean stepmothers, misbehaving children, financial woes, or terrorist attacks from another kingdom.

Those Sunday evening fairy tales held many similarities to the Sunday morning Bible stories. We saw Cinderella being rescued from the ashes to become a princess, and another princess cursed to sleep until awakened by her true love's kiss. Lo and behold, the heroine of our favorite fairy tale ate poisoned fruit too, except this time it was a wicked witch instead of a serpent doing all the talking. We saw handsome princes riding on white horses to rescue distressed damsels.

No one ever talked about the truth of those fairy tales unless one of us had nightmares. Then we were comforted and told that those stories weren't really true after all, but just *make-believe*, and that Jesus would take care of us if we were frightened because he was real.

Yet we were told that Santa Claus was real too, and so was the Easter Bunny, and if we were good little boys and girls who believed without question, we would get presents. So we believed those things until somewhere along the way one of our parents or an older sibling let us in on the secret. That it was all just ... *make-believe*.

In our little minds all the stories seemed the same, and quite honestly, all a bit far-fetched. After all, if Jesus could walk on water why couldn't a pumpkin turn into a beautiful carriage?

Wasn't prayer a bit like wishing upon a star? After all, didn't we pray to God in rhyme as well? *Now I lay me down to sleep, I pray the Lord my soul to keep....*

I don't know about you, but at my church, I heard that if I was

BEFORE I EVER MET MY HUSBAND, I WAS IN LOVE WITH A PRINCE WHO EXISTED ONLY IN MY IMAGINATION.

good, beautiful "on the inside," and loved Jesus with all my heart, he would save me and I'd go to heaven. But in the evenings in front of television I learned if I was good and beautiful on the outside and loved a man with all my heart, that man would rescue me, and I'd live happily ever after right here on earth. Since I was only six and heaven seemed very far away, the fairy tales I heard made far more practical sense to me than what I heard in church. After all, I sang songs about Jesus loving the little children, and me in particular, so why should I worry?

It seemed far more important to find a boyfriend than to find Jesus, at least according to the magazines my babysitter read and the commercials I saw on television. I figured I needed to worry about getting beautiful on the outside first and worry about the inside later, especially if I wanted to go to the prom, have a fabulous wedding, give birth to beautiful babies, buy that dream house ... and live happily ever after.

Though I really didn't understand what it meant to be beautiful on the inside, I knew exactly what it meant to be beautiful on the outside. I knew that I would have to work really hard at it if I was ever going to get to wear that magic slipper and ride on that white horse. All I saw in my ordinary mirror was a plump, short little girl with glasses—not exactly Magic Kingdom material, at least not in the books I'd read.

I longed for a Magic Mirror that would show me how to secure my future, teach me the secrets of life, and, best of all, transform me into a woman with the power to enchant a prince—a prince handsome and daring enough to whisk me away to that perfect life I believed was just on the other side.

NOT SO HAPPILY EVER AFTER

Of course, that didn't happen. But like a lot of young women, I clung to the fairy tale. Before I ever met my husband, I was in love with a prince who existed only in my imagination.

Like most women of my generation, I was told that my real purpose in life was to get married and have children. So at the ripe old age of twenty, I married a boy I met the summer before I went off to college. With no real life experience from which to draw, I never considered any other choices I might have, to tell the truth. All I knew was that we thought we were "in love." In retrospect, I know now that mainly what we had was a case of raging hormones. It took many years for the real love to begin.

After we married, I finished college as a day student and graduated with a degree in English. I tried to teach high school for a couple of years but hated it. Soon after deciding to pursue a career in counseling, I discovered I was pregnant with our son. So I delayed my career plans and gave birth to our son, and not long thereafter, our daughter. We had our children just as planned, in the right order, on schedule, and perfectly spaced two years apart.

I did have a difficult miscarriage in between the two children, but the loss just made me more determined to create the kind of home I'd always imagined. I vowed that as long as I was a wife and mother, I would work hard to create a happy home for my husband and children.

Those events completed, my husband and I focused on building our dream home. Our children and our business thrived, so we built a big house and joined the country club. I had great fun decorating, buying new furniture, and landscaping the spacious yard.

I volunteered in my community and started taking night classes at a local university, working toward a master's degree in counseling. We even started attending a Methodist church. I had been reared in a Presbyterian church and my husband was a Baptist, so we decided we would try a third alternative. Not that it mattered much—we weren't quite sure what we believed at that point in our lives. We just believed that going to church was the right thing to do.

My life was moving along right on schedule.

Our marriage seemed good—though my husband worked very long hours—and the children were well behaved and appeared well adjusted and happy. Eventually I completed my degree, but decided I would wait until the children were in grade school before I looked for a job. After all, my husband's business was doing well enough so that I didn't have to work, and day care was very expensive.

GOD HAS A WAY

OF USING ONE

CRISIS TO DIVERT

ANOTHER.

One day a friend invited me to a nearby women's fellowship where I shocked myself and accepted Christ as my Savior. I hadn't realized how spiritually hungry I had become and that, no matter how perfect my life seemed from the outside, there was something missing. My husband attended a Christian conference several months later and accepted Christ as well. For about a year our lives really did seem perfect.

But then the bottom fell out.

THE LONG WILDERNESS JOURNEY

The problems began when a recession hit the farming industry in 1981. In an effort to cut losses, we sold our farm and started a landscaping business, but the recession worsened and construction took a nose-dive. We had invested all our profits in heavy earth-moving equipment, but we had to sell it as the economy worsened.

I accepted a full-time job for the first time in my life, which was very stressful with two kids in elementary school. My husband traveled out of town a great deal pursuing large contracts and was rarely home for the children's activities. In addition, he became depressed because he missed farming so much.

I had no clinical training at that time, so I did not recognize his depression; I just thought he was tired and overworked. The more depressed he became, the more he distanced himself from the children and me. Resentful and lonely, I busied myself pursuing my own dreams and career. I turned to my music and my work as a kind of self-defense from the lonely nights when he would sleep in front of the television or shut himself up in his office doing paperwork. We drifted further and further apart.

We didn't talk about it, but we both realized we needed to do something before it was too late. In an effort to salvage our relationship and create more career opportunities for ourselves, we decided to sell our house and move closer to jobs and better schools for our children. But deep down, we both knew our marriage had reached a crossroads.

Counseling wasn't readily available in those days, and not as many people divorced either, especially in rural North Carolina. We knew that the logical time to separate, if we were going to do it, was then— when most of our assets were liquidated. We didn't even bother to fight anymore, and we barely spoke to each other for days on end.

We were both Christians, but by this time our commitment had worn thin. The stress of our emotional

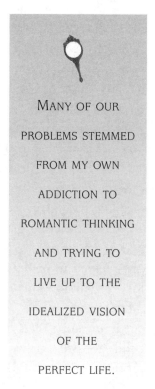

MANY OF OUR

PROBLEMS STEMMED

FROM MY OWN

ADDICTION TO

ROMANTIC THINKING

AND TRYING TO

LIVE UP TO THE

IDEALIZED VISION

OF THE

PERFECT LIFE.

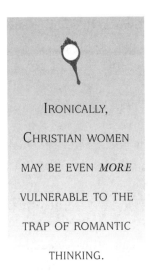

IRONICALLY,

CHRISTIAN WOMEN

MAY BE EVEN *MORE*

VULNERABLE TO THE

TRAP OF ROMANTIC

THINKING.

distance, financial difficulty, and the lack of a strong group of Christian friends who kept us accountable had taken its toll on our lives. We had drifted away and pursued our own dreams instead of being obedient to God. Thinking about those days still makes me sad.

But God has a way of using one crisis to divert another. Just when I thought I had the courage to tell my husband I wanted to end our marriage, on a beautiful spring day when I least expected it, I received a terrible phone call. It was someone from my husband's company calling to tell me Rick had collapsed on the job. He had been rushed to a local hospital emergency room where it was learned he was suffering from an ulcer, which had caused internal bleeding. However, the bleeding became life-threatening when a tube a doctor inserted into his stomach accidentally tore a hole in his esophagus. He had to be given seven pints of blood!

The news terrified me. Friends drove me to the hospital three hours away. When I got there, the doctors told me the bleeding had finally stopped, but Rick was still very weak.

I will never forget how he looked lying in that hospital bed and how all the tension and anger of the last two years just seemed to melt away. In that moment I remembered the love I had for him and knew this was the man God had intended for me.

I vowed to the Lord right then and there that if my husband got well, I would stay with him and work out the problems. Praise the Lord, Rick did get well.

It has been twenty years since that episode, and I have kept my promise. We've endured major financial struggles, job losses, the suicide of my young brother, a diagnosis of Type I diabetes for our son, and an estranged daughter. We've suffered, but I am grateful we have made it to this place. I've become a licensed marital and family therapist, and I love my work helping others through counseling and seminars. My husband and I have parented and worked with scores of children in foster care, and we've had the privilege of leading many to Christ and helping them heal from terrible life wounds. We have lived in unique places and met a lot of wonderful people. We have a good life.

But I'll be the first to admit many of our problems stemmed from my own addiction to romantic thinking and trying to live up to the idealized vision of the perfect life I imagined in my head. That vision drove me to expect way too much of my very human husband. Not only did I expect him to be handsome forever (actually, he is quite handsome) and to provide me with financial security, but I expected him to understand me totally and to anticipate all my needs. I became frightened when he wrestled with depression and when things we could not control happened to our business. Through it all, I expected him to be able to fill that empty place in my heart that always longed for *something more*.

I expected him to be my prince.

No wonder we almost divorced.

STARING IN THE MIRROR

Are you like me?

Have you struggled to reconcile the life you live with the life you've dreamed of having?

Did you get your hopes up because your husband actually attended Promise Keepers, but now the promises seem empty?

Perhaps you go to women's conferences and hear about faith and joy, but at home you cry when no one is looking. Has your doctor told you you're depressed? Maybe you're taking antidepressants, but you still can't seem to find joy in life. Have you gained weight over the past few years? Are you often too tired for sex? On the rare occasions when it does happen, do you enjoy it?

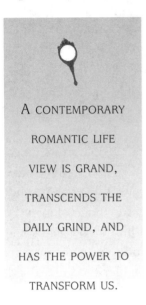

A CONTEMPORARY ROMANTIC LIFE VIEW IS GRAND, TRANSCENDS THE DAILY GRIND, AND HAS THE POWER TO TRANSFORM US.

Perhaps your husband doesn't seem attracted to you at all anymore, and you feel hurt and angry. But when you try to discuss your dissatisfaction with him he just turns over and tunes you out or says he doesn't know what is wrong between the two of you. You get angrier and he gets more distant.

Lonely, sad, and wondering how you got yourself in this mess, you hide in your bedroom eating junk food and reading romance novels (and fantasizing) while Prince Belchalot watches football and the children fight over the computer down the hall.

WELCOME TO LIFE IN THE MAGIC KINGDOM

You're not alone. Millions of women feel like you do. Sometimes it seems as if the whole world is trying desperately to sort through the confusion resulting from a half century of exposure to the false messages and romanticized thinking hidden so cleverly in marketing and entertainment.

Ironically, Christian women may be even *more* vulnerable to the trap of romantic thinking than non-Christians. After all, haven't we always been told that if we make our husbands and our children our first priority, and if we are good wives and mothers, we will be loved and cherished by our husbands and that our "children [will] rise up and call [us] blessed" (Prov. 31:28)?

In too many churches, Christian women have been trained to look good, act happy, and hide their problems. They have been taught to pretend. They have been made to feel that if they are unhappy it is because they are not praying hard enough or there is something wrong with them. As a result, they deny feelings of failure and unhappiness until it is too late and they're headed to divorce court. We may talk about our problems with some of our family and friends, but mostly it is to gripe and complain. We don't truly confide in anyone who can give us any real spiritual guidance until it is too late.

Even though we may not have affairs, develop serious addictions, or run off with our bosses, many of us spend our lives stuffing down disappointment and disillusionment with food, shopping, television, movies, and romance novels.

We continue to feed ourselves a steady diet of the very things that are killing us.

MORE THAN JUST ROMANCE

Romance, for the purposes of this book, describes more than the relationship between a man and a woman. It is a broader concept that describes a way of looking at everything in life.

The word *romance* entered language in the Middle Ages, probably in France, and ultimately meant "in the Roman manner." Romans were known for their style and grandiosity and their penchant for stretching the truth to entertain.

The word was used initially to describe tales told by itinerant bards as they traveled around the countryside providing entertainment for the masses. Stories in the romantic tradition were expected to be embellished, larger than life, and full of miracles and supernatural events. No one wanted stories about ordinary events. Folks wanted drama!

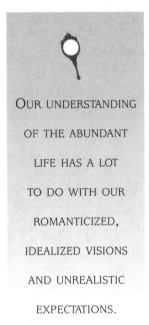

OUR UNDERSTANDING

OF THE ABUNDANT

LIFE HAS A LOT

TO DO WITH OUR

ROMANTICIZED,

IDEALIZED VISIONS

AND UNREALISTIC

EXPECTATIONS.

A contemporary romantic life view is grand, transcends the daily grind, and has the power to transform us into people who are heroic and legendary—at least for a short while. For women, that usually means becoming so beautiful we have the power to change a man's heart. If you think about it, the movies we all watched while growing up contain this same message: *If women are beautiful enough, not only can they change a man, but they can also change history.*

Isn't Beauty able to transform the Beast? Doesn't Cinderella rise out of the ashes and change tradition by enchanting the prince so much that he marries a commoner?

But here's the problem: Even though many women long for an extraordinary life, we don't want to do extraordinary things to get it. We are afraid to step out into the world and make that life happen for ourselves, so we look for a mate who will. And if all we desire is to be a wife and mother, once we get this, for many of us, it doesn't seem to be enough. We want more. The problems start when the man we marry isn't able to give us the life we hoped he would, so we spend our days trying to change him into the kind of man who will.

When that fails we run to our mirrors to see if we can figure out why. We go to church looking for peace, but all we can focus on is the supposedly perfect family sitting in the pew in front of us. We secretly envy our thin neighbor because she has perky breasts, perfect hair, and a husband who dotes on her. Not only that, but she has a promising music ministry traveling with a high-powered evangelist.

We're shocked when we discover this same woman ran off with that evangelist and the perfect Christian couple divorces. How could someone who appeared to have all the ingredients for a magical life not be happy?

Our hearts are dying. Without any real understanding of how to deal with our confusion and unfulfilled longings, we try to turn to God. But usually it is to beg God to give us what we think we need. We may ask God to give us the kind of marriage that leads us closer to him and the "abundant life," but we don't realize that our idea of abundance is more material than spiritual. Our understanding of the abundant life has a lot to do with our romanticized, idealized visions and unrealistic expectations. So when we find ourselves married to a man who doesn't make us feel powerful like that irritating Proverbs 31 woman or loved and cherished like that little nymph described in the Song of Solomon, we wonder what is wrong with us. The only conclusions we can come to are that

1. we were not special enough to attract the right man;
2. we married the wrong man;
3. our husbands need to change.

So we tell ourselves we'll pray harder, look more beautiful, keep a cleaner house, and be kinder and more loving. Then we volunteer for more committees and join the choir.

Yeah! That's it. We'll get more spiritual and that will change him!

Outwardly, we seem to be on the right track. Inwardly, we're wondering if there's a contingency clause in the marriage contract regarding "submission"—particularly if we can prove to ourselves our husbands are hopeless dolts.

Knowing how fast gossip spreads, we're terrified to confide in our Christian friends. And many of them seem so spiritual, we figure if we opened up about our shameful thoughts and checkered pasts, they'd point those well-manicured fingers at us and the floor would swallow us up whole. We couldn't dare tell them about our painful experiences in adolescence, the rejections, our present longings, and secret fantasies.

So we hide behind our masks and pretend to be wise and spiritual too, vowing that this time things are going to be different. After all, if we wish and pretend and pray long enough, surely all of our dreams will come true, right? We'll be transformed into the kind of woman our husbands will adore, and in return, he'll be transformed into the kind of husband who will fulfill all of our romantic visions.

In other words, we employ *magical thinking*.

CHAPTER TWO

WHEN YOU WISH UPON A STAR

Now all wept and mourned for her; but He said,
"Do not weep; she is not dead, but sleeping."

—Luke 8:52

*S*ince we are so good at pretending, let's pretend we actually did go to that women's conference. Imagine the topic was something like "Making Your Christian Hubby Happy."

Oh, dear.

You arrive home terribly late to a house that is dark and cold. You almost break your neck because your husband forgot to turn on the porch light for you. You walk in the back door and fumble to find the light switch. The first thing you see is trash spilling out of the garbage can and the sink piled high with dirty dishes. A pot of burned spaghetti sits on the stove. The milk carton sits on the counter, half empty and sour. With a sinking spirit you realize that you will have to go to the grocery store in the morning, but you don't have any money. In all your excitement you spent your last few dollars for the week on a set of teaching tapes you bought at the conference.

You had fantasized that he would greet you at the door with a passionate kiss. But he's asleep on the couch and doesn't even realize you've gotten home. You try to rouse him from his stupor and tell him how much you missed him, but he has garlic on his breath from the spaghetti, and instead of kissing you back, he yawns and asks where you put the Tums as he shuffles down the hall to the bedroom, scratching himself through his undershirt.

So much for that passionate, romantic greeting you'd been anticipating for hours. After all, weren't you all primed to practice what you learned at the conference?

You feel rejected. You know you could pray and read the Bible, but the dirty kitchen is really bothering you even though it's very late. After all, you did all that spiritual stuff at the conference anyway.

You wash the dishes and bag up the trash, but you really start to get angry when you have to pick up cereal bowls off the floor in the den. On top of that, when you check the mail, you discover your husband forgot to pay an overdue bill you'd asked him to mail while you were gone.

Where is that peace that passes all understanding when you need it?

How come that bozo can't even take out the trash?

Fuming, you undress and crawl into your side of the bed, as far away from your husband as you can get, with tears sliding down your face from fatigue, confusion, and disappointment.

What happened? Was that stupid trip just a total waste of time and money?

The days go by, and you forget the things you vowed at the conference to try. The teaching tapes you bought get crammed into the back of a desk drawer or are lost underneath the car seat. You make more lunch dates with your friends (who are also discontented), read another romance novel, and buy another dress for that next social affair you are planning. You change your hair color and sign up for another Bible study, but quit going after the first two or three sessions because you don't have time to do the homework. You're teaching Sunday school, chairing the Arts Festival, and hosting twenty couples from church for a barbecue next Saturday night. Besides that, the study doesn't seem relevant to your life.

You have your barbecue. But when it's over, you're tired, depressed, and deeper in debt from the cost of all that food. Your husband seemed to connect with a few of the guys, but nothing comes of it, which depresses you further. If he doesn't join the men's group at church, how will he ever see how a real Christian husband is supposed to act? He's not a bad guy—he goes to church every Sunday—but he's his same ordinary self the rest of the week. He's boring, predictable, and cares more about the television and the football game than he does about you, right?

MANY WOMEN I COUNSEL ADMIT THEY JUST YEARN FOR SOMETHING MORE.

Maybe if you can just go to the next marriage conference that's coming up in a few weeks, God will change your husband into the man he needs to be—a man who will make you feel beautiful and special; a man who will understand your emotional needs. Maybe he'll finally turn into a man who will give you the "happily ever after" your heart has always desired.

ALWAYS WANTING SOMETHING MORE

Grown women know the difference between fairy tales and Bible stories. We know there is no prince who will rescue us and change our lives forever. Surely we know there is no "happily ever after," at least on this side of heaven.

Don't we?

I'm not sure we do—at least not in the deep parts of our brains that control our emotions and our most primitive core responses to stressful life events.

By now, many of you have tasted a good deal more than your fair share of heartache and pain, and you've learned that life is just plain hard. Perhaps you gave up on finding a prince a long time ago, or you thought you had married him but he turned out to be a toad. Maybe he was a dark prince and dumped you—out of the blue—for another damsel in distress.

WHEN WE ARE

THINKING MAGICALLY,

WE ARE NOT

THINKING CLEARLY.

But most men are not that bad. Many women I counsel admit they just yearn for something more, even though their lives seem quite good by most standards. They are bored, lonely, and feel empty inside. They wonder if they married the right man. Though they wouldn't dream of having an affair or divorcing, they fantasize a great deal about what their lives would be like if their husbands were more romantic, more attentive, or more successful by worldly standards. Many feel as if they have nothing in common with their husbands at all. They dream of a "soul mate" who will anticipate all their needs. Try as they might, they can't shake the idea that life is supposed to be different and that another man might be the answer.

Even while they are pretending to the world that everything is just fine.

THE MIRROR AS METAPHOR

The Magic Mirror is a metaphor for the illusions we harbor in our hearts about how life is supposed to be. The voices that speak to us from that mirror are our critical parents, our carnal friends, the media, and our own selfish wills. The longer we harbor those illusions, the more we tend to indulge in "magical thinking," a term well known by therapists. When we are thinking magically, we are not thinking clearly. Our thoughts are not based on truth and therefore our life choices are often misguided, if not downright wrong. Those choices cause us to become "trapped."

ONLY GOD HAS THE POWER TO MAKE YOU FEEL GOOD ABOUT YOURSELF.

I've identified five major falsehoods that form the underlying belief systems of women who are "trapped in the mirror" and thinking magically about life and marriage. But don't be misled—you don't have to believe all five of these falsehoods to qualify. Just one of these persistent little bugs can be enough to throw your life out of balance. Think of it like a computer with a virus. Just one tiny "worm" can mess up the whole system.

THE FATAL FIVE FALSEHOODS

1. If I strive to be beautiful, sexually attractive, and successful by the standards of the world, my husband will be entranced by me. This will make me feel good about myself and I will bask in the reflected glory of his love.

REAL LOVE MEANS

ACCEPTING PEOPLE

AS THEY ARE.

2. If my husband really loves me, he will change into the man I need him to be.

3. If my husband doesn't treat me well, God has forgotten me.

4. If I love others more than I love myself, they will need me. Being needed will make me feel loved. I must always put the needs of others first.

5. If bad things happen to me or if I don't have the desires of my heart, there must be something wrong with me.

I call the beliefs above *fatal* because they can slowly strangle a relationship without a woman even knowing what is happening. They are poisonous beliefs.

THE REAL TRUTHS

These are the answers to the falsehoods listed above. I call them the Fabulous Five.

1. Your husband cannot make you feel good about yourself if you don't feel good about yourself already. Only God has the power to make you feel good about yourself. A husband does not have the power to rescue you from the cinders and turn you into a princess. You must bask in God's reflected glory. If you do not feel beautiful in God's eyes, you will never feel beautiful in your husband's eyes.

2. Real love means accepting people as they are, and

not expecting any person to change to make you happy. You can pray they will change for their own good, but not for yours.

3. God has not abandoned you, even when your husband doesn't treat you well. If you turn to God, he can work in the situation for your good.

4. Being needed is not to be confused with being loved. A person exhibiting true love strives to help the other person to be less needy by encouraging individual spiritual and emotional growth. But it does not mean that you always put the other's needs first by not treating yourself well. You must love your neighbor (husband, child, etc.) as you love yourself—not more than you love yourself.

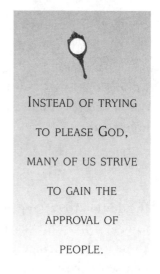

INSTEAD OF TRYING TO PLEASE GOD, MANY OF US STRIVE TO GAIN THE APPROVAL OF PEOPLE.

5. God does not give you the desires of your heart unless your heart is fixed on him. He changes your heart to line up with his will. Denying you what you want may be the most loving thing God does for you. God doesn't reward you for being good by giving you everything you want.

Husbands do not change because *we* want them to. They change because *they* want to. The key to turning a man's heart to God and motivating him to change is loving and appreciating him as he is.

As to worth, God does not want his children to be insecure and performance-oriented. But instead of trying to please God, many of us strive to gain the approval of people. We do this because we're addicted to the attention and positive affirmation that goes along with approval, especially from our husbands.

WE ALWAYS WANT SOMETHING MORE.

The huge underlying lie that fuels the Fatal Five is that we are not worthy as women unless we are beautiful, sexy, intelligent, successful, and a man adores us.

The world constantly feeds us that false message and most of us have swallowed it whole. Measuring our worth by the world's standards—instead of God's—is like trying to nourish our bodies on candy. We're never full, never satisfied, never nourished.

WISHING, HOPING, DREAMING

In addition to seeking approval from our husbands, we also try to gain it from other women. We want their approval, and we know we have achieved that when we have inspired their envy. Our sense of self-worth becomes dependent on feeling as if we have outdone them. Heaven help us if we feel they have outdone us.

To achieve this, we strive for perfect homes, thin bodies, and impeccable makeup. We stare at our images in the mirror, searching for areas to improve so our husbands will love us and other women will feel jealous of us. We binge, purge, pluck, tweeze, starve, paint, decorate, take classes, start hobbies, spend, shop, flirt, fantasize, get facelifts and injections, take pills, cry, order exercise equipment, build houses, have more babies, plan parties, then start all over again—all in a quest for that *something more*. After a while, our needing turns into craving, and when we crave something—anything—we don't control it, our craving controls us. We are enslaved to it. We become addicted to an endless narcissistic cycle of perfectionism and attention-seeking in order to feel worthy and valued, and it is our husbands who bear the burdens of our cravings. Even when we do get attention from our husbands, we're startled to discover it's not enough.

We always want something more.

TRAPPED IN THE MAGIC MIRROR

Entrapment has a thousand different faces. Some women become addicted to diet pills or develop anorexia or bulimia. Some max out all their credit cards and file bankruptcy. Others begin flirting with a coworker, and eventually, though the relationship seemed beautiful and special in the beginning, they realize they're caught in a sordid, painful affair. Some women develop addictions to alcohol or pain pills. They may shoplift or gamble. In an effort to sexually arouse their husbands, wives might join their husbands in watching pornography. At first it seems like innocent, harmless fun, but eventually he's impotent without it—and neither husband nor wife can understand how things got so out of control.

THE DREAM YOU SEE IN THAT MIRROR IS AN ILLUSION.

Yet women continue to stare into the mirror, holding on to the magical belief that if they are just good enough, pray more, and work harder at being a perfect wife, everything will change, especially their husbands.

The Magic Mirror doesn't always lead to some huge disaster. Sometimes it leads women into a barren, dead-end wilderness of depression and a kind of life I call the "silent scream." Or, like Snow White, they go to sleep (metaphorically) until some man rescues them. For many women, this kind of life is a daily reality. Some of these women sit next to you in church. That woman may even be you.

The dream you see in that mirror is an illusion. It presents itself as a Magical Kingdom where life seems exciting, you feel confident, and you're free from any kind of pain—if you could only figure out how to get through that glass.

The reality, however, is that it's a place full of pain, heartache, shame, and guilt. It stinks of death.

Eve was a magical thinker. She let herself believe she could have it all if she just ate that forbidden fruit. Her curiosity turned into a narcissistic need, and then that need turned into a craving. Eventually, it cost her the garden.

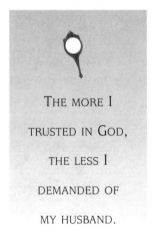

THE MORE I TRUSTED IN GOD, THE LESS I DEMANDED OF MY HUSBAND.

There really is a wicked queen (and you know who her daddy is) whose entire existence depends on getting us to eat that poisoned apple and trapping us in the mirror so we get lost in the wilderness on the other side. Not only do we take daily bites, but we occasionally make apple pie out of it, and we frequently feed poisoned applesauce to our children as well.

The Magic Mirror makes me angry. In fact, I'd like to take a great big old sledgehammer and shatter that awful gob of glass into a million pieces. Like many of you, I have friends and relatives who've had tragic histories with men. They married because they were madly "in love" and were willing to sacrifice everything and anybody in the name of love. Inevitably, when their husbands abandoned or abused them, some emotionally abandoned their children. Some subjected their families to raging conflict and bitter tension. Some became alcoholics or turned suicidal.

As a professional therapist I've seen hundreds of children's lives ruined by their parents' romantic escapades—neglected because their parents are too focused on their own romantic dramas. Just ask any social worker in Child Protective Services these days. The problem transcends all races, social classes, and religions. I've dealt with many parents in my career who've appeared as upstanding Christians in their communities, but had, in actuality, come to me because they had been charged by the state with neglect. Most of this neglect stemmed from conflict caused by divorce, custody issues, fights over visitation, competition between ex-spouses, and emotional abandonment caused by parents caring more about their new love interests than about their own children.

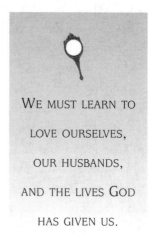

WE MUST LEARN TO
LOVE OURSELVES,
OUR HUSBANDS,
AND THE LIVES GOD
HAS GIVEN US.

My own personal history testifies to the power of entrapment.

I don't know exactly when I stepped into the mirror myself. I know, in part, the realization came as my children began to grow up and I had to face the ways in which my own confusion and lack of understanding about these things had adversely affected their spiritual health and development into mature adults.

I learned a great deal more as I began counseling women and seeing their mistakes in the light of my own experiences. It took years for my thoughts to solidify and for me to understand just how superficial and shallow my Christianity had been and how much my marriage and my children had suffered because of it. But unfortunately, I didn't learn much of this until after my children were grown up and out in the world on their own. I know now that I didn't spend enough time thinking about their needs because I was too busy trying to grow up myself and attempting to deal with my own idealized vision of how life should be instead of how it actually was. I was torn between feeling totally inadequate and striving for perfection.

But it is never too late to change. Little by little, as I turned to Christ and allowed him to work in my heart, I began to see him—rather than my husband—as my source. Oddly enough, the more I trusted in God, the less I demanded of my husband. And the less I demanded of my husband, the more Christlike he became.

He is not my prince. He is just a very good husband. Jesus is the only one worthy of the title of Prince.

We must learn to overcome our romanticized worldview. For the sake of our children, we must learn to love ourselves, our husbands, and the lives God has given us.

But as simple as that sounds, there are many physical, emotional, and spiritual dynamics we need to understand before we can see how that simple truth works. Some of the simplest truths are the most profound and the most difficult to incorporate into our everyday living.

One of the first things we have to understand is how our biology as women predisposes us to romantic addiction, how wounds from our adolescence make us more vulnerable to confusion and the development of false belief systems, and the way our culture, even the church, enables that process.

WHERE DID THEY PUT THAT FAIRY DUST?

For the weapons of our warfare are not carnal
but mighty in God for pulling down strongholds, casting
down arguments and every high thing that exalts
itself against the knowledge of God, bringing every thought
into captivity to the obedience of Christ.

—2 Corinthians 10:4–5

I might bang the drum a bit too much if I begin this chapter with a discussion of how bad most television seems these days, or how biblically unsound. So I won't beat that drum.

Well ... maybe just a little bit.

In order for us to understand how we become trapped, I need to address just exactly *how* secular programming causes us to form irrational and false beliefs about life. This begins early in our childhood. Remember in the first chapter how I entered into the Magic Kingdom every Sunday evening? How many times as a child did you and I "wish upon a star"? Did you know that every time we did this, an irrational belief became more deeply ingrained in our little brains?

It all seems quite harmless, but let's look at how a child's brain forms and the process that makes all children vulnerable to false thought formation to some degree or other. I think you'll be surprised.

The child I am concerned about in this book is *you*—or at least the child you used to be—and how your thinking then has affected who you are now. Even though you're all grown up now and consider yourself experienced and knowledgeable about life, your addiction to romantic thinking started years ago.

You may think the problem is specific to women who grew up before the feminist movement in America and that contemporary women are less vulnerable to romantic thinking. You might even believe that, because traditional feminine role expectations are not as rigid and women are better educated, most of us understand that the June Cleavers of the world are imaginary.

If you really believe that, just turn on your television for a little while. One quick foray into primetime television is all it takes to understand the scope of the problem. In spite of the feminist movement, higher paying jobs, and better educations, romantic thinking is alive and well. In fact, I'd say we are more in bondage to it than ever. Today the fairy tales have been contemporized in books and movies like *Ella Enchanted* and *The Princess Diaries*. Not only are we seemingly more obsessed with romance, but that romantic vision exploits our sexuality more than it did when I was growing up, which makes the possibilities for destruction that much greater.

Although you know the definition of romantic thinking and the falsehoods on which it is based, it is the *roots* of this thinking that drive our problems. God wants us to put the "ax to the roots" (see Matt. 3:10) so we kill the tree in our minds that bears the fruit of poisonous belief. If we don't, it just springs up like a weed somewhere else in our lives.

THE CHILD'S GROWING BRAIN

Very little research has focused on studying romantic content in children's programming or how it relates to an addiction to romantic thinking in adulthood. Unlike violent or graphically sexual content, which has been studied in great depth, romanticism in children's literature is relatively uncharted territory. Part of the reason seems to be that romantic thinking has not been identified by scientific communities as a problem. For there to be funding for research, problems have to be identified. That's regrettable, because I suspect that if we looked at the issue more seriously, a good deal less teen pregnancy, abortion, and divorce might happen in the long run.

We know from research that children exposed to highly sexual visual content are at greater risk for developing many problems. They become sexually active earlier, are at greater risk for teen pregnancy, and are at higher risk for sexually-transmitted disease. If you are interested, the Web site www.protectkids.com gives reference to a number of studies about this topic. Likewise, children exposed to violence in their childhoods are more likely to exhibit aggressive behaviors themselves. They are more likely to be convicted of a serious crime than children not exposed to violence, and they are at great risk for becoming victims of a criminal act themselves (Office of Juvenile Justice and Delinquency Prevention [1997] *Bulletin*, Washington, DC).

But because romantic content is viewed as relatively innocent and fun, normal and natural, the generally accepted opinion seems to be that the presence of a romantic story in a child's program is benign. Just about every G- or PG-rated movie out there these days contains a love story of some kind—even the story lines with animals as the main characters!

I find problems with that assumption. Neuroscience has proven that the information we see and hear repeatedly as children causes the formation of new neural pathways as our young brains develop. Each new thing we learn as a child, even if it is an exaggeration or a falsehood, creates a new neural connection. These connections eventually form a web of trillions of neural pathways by the time we walk and talk. The more that information and experience is repeated, the stronger and *the more permanent* those neural pathways become. A neural pathway that becomes permanent becomes a *mind-set*, and mind-sets are very difficult to change. In fact, mind-sets based on falsehoods that drive adult thinking are called *strongholds* in Christian psychology. (See 2 Cor. 10:4–5.)

In other words, our most primitive emotional responses and beliefs about life are laid down very early in childhood, and the more they are reinforced by experience, the more deeply rooted they become. In fact, most child development experts agree that basic character and personality formation occurs in children by the age of six or seven.

There is another key component. Research suggests that the *information we see and hear at the same time* (such as movies or television) becomes the information most deeply encoded, with the most impact, the longest lasting, and the most difficult to change. Those messages go so deep they don't just form the basis of opinion, they become part of who we are. You can explain all you want to children that those things they see are fantasy, but deep inside they will operate on what they've learned from hearing and seeing as younger children—not what you tell them is true later in their lives.

Doesn't it make sense that too much exposure to romantic content at a young age could have the same negative impact on marriage that exposure to violence has on criminal behavior? Even if the correlation between the two is not as measurable, doesn't it make a good deal of sense to limit the amount of romantic fantasy to which your child is exposed?

I am not a research scientist and I do not claim to have conducted studies under carefully controlled conditions to determine the accuracy of my opinions, so please do not think that I am putting them forth as scientific fact. They are opinions, nothing more and nothing less. I would welcome evidence to the contrary.

However, I've talked to hundreds of women through the years and heard the same references to the "fairy-tale life" enough times that I believe God has shown me some important and fundamental concepts. A number of therapists and researchers are doing excellent work in the field of neuroscience of romance. But my work is specifically targeted to the Christian woman and how romantic addiction affects not only her marital satisfaction, but her overall feelings about herself and her relationship with God as well. That is difficult to test by scientific standards.

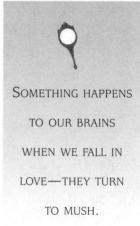

SOMETHING HAPPENS TO OUR BRAINS WHEN WE FALL IN LOVE—THEY TURN TO MUSH.

If you are parenting a young child, I hope you give this some serious thought. But what I really want you to think about is your own childhood, especially if you had no spiritual training to offset what you saw and heard as a child. This is even more important if your spiritual training was confused because your parents were involved in New Age practices, the occult, or neopaganism, as often those belief systems attempt to justify abortion, sexual immorality, and perversion of all kinds. In the chapter about the wounds we suffer in adolescence, I'll discuss how "deficit parenting" affects the problem as well.

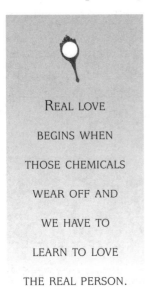

REAL LOVE BEGINS WHEN THOSE CHEMICALS WEAR OFF AND WE HAVE TO LEARN TO LOVE THE REAL PERSON.

What strongholds and mind-sets may have been laid down at the root level of your thinking? I'd like you to consider which things you learned as a child that might be causing you to have needs and desires you do not understand.

When I talk to women and we apply the Magic Mirror concepts to their personal lives, I'm amazed at the results. Without a doubt women are set free. As I teach these principles, they begin to see the fallacies in their thinking. They start to relate their depression, yearnings, and unhappiness back to the fantasies they formed about life when they were little girls. Then bit by bit, I help them unravel how their false thinking influences their views of themselves and the choices they make now. The focus of therapy redirects them away from their dissatisfaction with their husbands to their dissatisfaction with themselves. And that is where the real work and healing begins.

THE LUST FOR FAIRY DUST

The healing process involves more than just our thinking. If you have fallen in love before, you know exactly what I am talking about. Something happens to our brains when we fall in love—they turn to mush.

God designed all human beings this way, women especially, and the biochemical process is both elegant and efficient. Granted, there are many people, both men and women, who seem to control the process better than others. But by and large, we are designed to fall in love. This is God's design for procreation. Procreation requires us to want to engage in sex. Our brains cooperate by flooding our systems with chemicals that arouse us sexually. It is this flooding that causes us to feel romantic. The problem starts when we confuse chemistry with spirituality and relationship.

Real love begins when those chemicals wear off and we have to learn to love the real person instead of the person we fell in love with when that process was first initiated.

These chemicals are the reason we can't think clearly when we fall in love. They make us deaf, dumb, and blind so we won't stop and think too hard about what we are doing. Mother Nature (our flesh) wants to keep us stupid so we will fall "in love" with the first sexy guy that comes along, have sex with him, and get pregnant just as soon as possible. God wants us to pick an appropriate mate and marry him first.

But how do these chemicals work?

In order to understand how, you must first know that we are all programmed with an instinctual God-given drive to keep the human race alive by having children. We all, except for a few rare individuals, produce chemicals within our bodies that create desires within us to mate and bear children. Of course, it helps the process along to be sexually aroused.

The way your brain works to arouse you sexually is to pump out hormones whenever a suitable male comes around—and your DNA can actually tell when that is happening. In fact, your DNA acts kind of like a sophisticated radar system. It does not care whether the male is really attractive (although we all know that certainly helps), whether the timing is appropriate, or whether either one of you is married or has children already.

In fact, the more practice you have in the procreation process, the more attuned your body is to the mating signals, so having had children or being married is not a protective factor. The Bible warns us that we "war within our members" (see James 4:1) and that we should avoid all appearances of evil. If we get ourselves into compromising situations, then the biochemical process will begin, and regardless of how strong or pure we think ourselves to be, we will be vulnerable. In addition, our sin nature will fight our spirit tooth and nail, finding every reason in the world to justify giving in to the temptation. No one is immune to it, and if you think you are, then you are being set up for a fall. Once the process starts, stopping it is like trying to slow down a freight train traveling at full speed.

WE ALL REMEMBER THE FIRST TIME WE REALLY FELL IN LOVE.

What are those chemicals? Pat Love explained the process in great detail in her book *The Truth About Love* (Fireside, 2001, 28–29), but I've given you a shortened version in the footnote below, paraphrased from her book.† I don't want to get sidetracked by too much technical information here, but I can't stress enough how important it is for you to recognize that addictive, euphoric, lying feeling.

---

† The primary chemicals responsible for the feeling of falling in love are PEA, norepinephrines, and dopamine. Dr. Helen Fisher at Rutgers University in New Jersey has also completed some compelling studies in the last few years that show that there are major differences in the brain scans of men and women who report themselves to be in the initial stages of a romantic relationship. It is not surprising that women's brain scans reveal more brain activity associated with reward, attention, and emotion, whereas men's reveal more activitiy associated with sexual arousal.

Unfortunately, many women confuse the process with feelings of intense spirituality. These are the women who believe that anything that feels so right can't possibly be wrong. That confusion has led some into bad marriages and sabotaged other perfectly good Christian marriages.

I've known married men and women caught up in extramarital affairs who've convinced themselves that because they felt so wonderful with another person, God actually sent that person to help them leave their spouses. God will never lead you into infidelity as an escape from an unhappy marriage. He may make a way for you to end an abusive marriage, but he will not send another sexual love interest to do so. Only Satan sends those kinds of emissaries.

We all remember the first time we really fell in love. We lost weight, couldn't sleep, and felt like we could conquer the world. But then we gradually settled down, and other feelings began to take the place of the initial euphoria. Those wonderful hormones started waning.

For those who marry, that process is usually over by the two-year mark, and the "falling in love" stage we experienced pretty much bottomed out. In other words, we returns to being normal. Living together prior to marriage does not prevent that process either.

Unfortunately, many couples assume that when the chemical soup goes sour, that means they're no longer in love. This belief has even more power when a woman is addicted to that euphoric feeling, needs it in order to feel good about herself, and is anxious and unhappy when her need for romance and excitement is no longer being met by her husband. This is when we are most likely to start eating for comfort and looking for ways to relieve the boredom and anxiety that begins to bubble in the secret places of our hearts.

Arguments escalate. Power struggles ensue. We wonder if it

was a mistake to marry. We look at our mates and wonder what ever drew us together. We cannot imagine spending the rest of our lives with that person.

Quite honestly, men are just as addicted to romance as women, but not because of the emotional excitement. They are addicted to the intensity of the sexual experience that results. The two-year mark for a marriage is often the time when men who are not strong in their relationship with God and committed to monogamy, and who deeply crave sexual intensity will initiate affairs with other women. Certain narcissistic men will continue that pattern throughout marriage. Men often confuse intense sexual feelings with real love.

Unfortunately, this is often the very time women choose to become pregnant in order to fill that empty space created by anxiety about their husband's waning attention and the loss of the romantic experience. But a baby doesn't fill up the space created by a lack of positive self-love, yearning for excitement, and that euphoric "falling in love" feeling. Flirting with other men, becoming anorexic, or filling up a closet full of clothes and shoes doesn't solve the problem either.

Still, we long for another exciting event that will make us feel like we did when we first fell in love. And that is the subject of the next chapter.

CHAPTER FOUR

THE BIG EVENT

We urge you, brethren, that you increase more and more;
that you also aspire to lead a quiet life, to mind your own
business, and to work with your own hands.

—1 Thessalonians 4:10–11

I love thrift stores. In fact, just about everything I wear, and most of what decorates my house, comes from a thrift store—or at least from end-of-season sales racks.

A lot of people don't believe me, but it's true. I don't remember exactly when I started, but through the years, I've turned thrift shopping into a fine art. I've found all the stores where wealthy socialites take their castoffs, and I've learned when to go in order to get the best bargains. As a result, I've filled my closet with name-brand clothes purchased for just a fraction of their original cost, most of which I bought with the tags still on them. I love the thrill of the hunt, especially when I nab a still-stylish $200 wool suit for just $20.

I frequently wonder about the history of items, especially those sequined ball gowns and used wedding dresses I always see hanging in the store. Many are quite elegant and you can tell they were expensive when new. Most look as if they were never worn at all. I can often imagine a beautiful girl dancing the night away in that dress, feeling like a princess. I can see her twirling on the dance floor, fairy lights sparkling on the balcony as the band plays a waltz. But then the cynic in me chuckles. The memory couldn't have been so wonderful if the dress ended up at a thrift store, now could it?

BIG EVENTS ARE THOSE SPECIAL OCCASIONS BY WHICH WE WOMEN MARK OUR LIVES.

Don't we normally keep those things to which we attach great importance? After all, I've dragged my thirty-six-year-old wedding dress around all these years and it is yellow and dry-rotted. I'm saving it for the grandchildren to play dress-up in, I suppose, if I ever have any. But those dresses in the thrift store were discarded with hardly any wear. Surely they were bought for someone's Big Event.

Whenever I see a wedding dress on the thrift store rack, I wonder if it belonged to someone who is now divorced. Statistics indicate that half of all marriages don't last. I'll bet the girls wished they'd spent that money on something more durable than a wedding dress. And the prom dresses—are the girls now grown and thirty pounds heavier? Is that why they got rid of the dresses—so they wouldn't have to be reminded of how happy they used to be?

PLANNING FOR THE BIG EVENT

Big Events are what I call those special occasions by which we women mark our lives. These huge, dramatically staged occasions allow us to be the center of attention and attain perfection, if only for a brief moment in time. They usually involve months of planning, lots of daydreaming, and certainly spending tons of money.

But for what?

Not only are these events staged with a great deal more frequency these days and at an earlier age for most women, but also they get bigger and more elaborate with each passing year.

At this point in time, my office is located above a women's clothing store. A children's beauty pageant boutique dominates the rear of the shop. Thankfully, the costumes are fairly modest and not as extreme as those often peddled to mothers with less discrimination. But the oddness of my office location doesn't fail to escape my attention. The irony is that upstairs I teach about not becoming obsessed with beauty and the Magic Mirror, while downstairs little girls parade in front of people so they can be judged on whether or not they are beautiful enough.

BIG EVENTS

ACTUALLY DON'T

CHANGE A THING.

What kind of message is this sending to our children? And what happens to a beauty queen when she runs out of Big Events? I suppose I never quite got over the JonBenet Ramsey murder, and I hope I never do. I haven't met anyone who could discuss it without expressing sadness, but also a great deal of distaste for the lifestyle at the same time. It's a mistake to have little girls dress up and pretend to be adults too early in life. Too much emphasis on this type of narcissistic activity can set the stage for later difficulty with ordinary life. Little girls like this go into adulthood absolutely convinced that life is no fun without a new dress or a constant stream of parties.

Growing up too fast also often means women crash and burn at an earlier age—that age when they realize the Big Events actually don't change a thing, and the prince is not going to show up to rescue them after all. What a terrible feeling for a young woman raised on a steady diet of "dress up." There comes a time, usually around midlife, when a woman realizes she is just an ordinary girl after all. She'll never be Cinderella and there are no more big parties in the works. The guy who was supposed to be a prince is getting bald, he likes to hunt and fish all the time, and he forgets their anniversary every year. On top of that, he shows up late for every function she wants him to attend. When he does get there, he talks too loudly and flirts too freely.

BIG EVENTS

DON'T MAKE

US HAPPY.

But some women just keep right on dealing in fantasy. They plan another Big Event to keep from having to think about the lack of true richness and meaning in their lives.

BIG EVENTS BEGIN EARLY

Children's beauty pageants aside, for most people it starts with the Junior Prom, although I've heard recently about schools beginning the process in elementary school.

It is not unusual for proms to start as early as the seventh grade now and for the girls to attend them looking like they are eighteen. I've heard that even for their younger children, parents are hiring limousines and treating the young couples to dinners at four-star restaurants. Ironically, the girls usually tower at least a foot taller than the boys, who all have acne and squeaky voices. I imagine these events usually cost around $500 before they are all over, but who even remembers them once they get to high school and move to the Senior Prom, which is nothing other than a much bigger version of the Junior Prom? The dresses cost more and a big party follows. For those with more affluent parents, there's a week at the beach to top off the festivities. For the *really* affluent, it is not unusual for that beach to be somewhere in the Caribbean.

The tradition continues through college. It starts with the Indian Summer Ball, the Harvest Ball, the Holly Ball, the Valentine's Ball, the Snow Ball, the Military Ball, and the Spring Ball. It wraps up with the Graduation Ball and all the parties and beach trips that follow.

Years ago, when my own daughter was in the ninth grade, I succumbed to the pressure to allow her to go to the prom with a junior in high school, the son of one of my friends.

He was a nice boy who didn't drink, and they weren't romantically attached at all. She begged to go. At that age, often rather awkward for many teen girls, she was quite the exception. Not only was she beautiful, but she looked much older than her years. We made sure our daughter understood this was not really a date, and when we felt she understood, we said yes.

I took her shopping and bought a little purple sequin dress that fit her to a tee. I spent about $200 that I couldn't really afford on the dress, accessories, and shoes—but she looked gorgeous.

Can you imagine my disappointment when she came home from the prom and all she could talk about was how her date never talked or danced (he was probably terrified), how bored she'd been, and how much she wished she hadn't gone?

So much for creating the Big Event that would make her happy.

I look back at those pictures now and I cringe. She is still beautiful, but I realize that the dress made her look way too old for her age. I should have said no to the prom until she was at least sixteen, and stuck to my decision. That was one of the lessons I learned the hard way. I wanted my daughter to be happy and believed that fulfilling her wishes would do just that.

Obviously, I was wrong. But in a way, I'm glad she didn't have a good time, because I think the incident taught us both a valuable lesson: Big Events don't make us happy.

Weddings Turn into Big Events

We all know the wedding is the really Big Event that most girls believe will transform their lives. It's the big day when all eyes are on the bride and no expense is spared to turn her into the beautiful princess she always wanted to be.

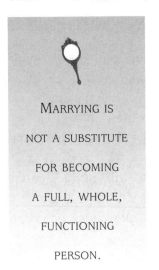

Marrying is not a substitute for becoming a full, whole, functioning person.

As a marriage therapist, I question if there is a direct correlation between the expense of the wedding and the failure of the marriage. Personally, I believe that when too much emphasis is placed on staging the wedding, then not enough time and energy is spent figuring out whether or not you really are right for each other and if God has called you to marry.

Outside of not choosing a good man to begin with, there are four common, terrible mistakes women often make when planning a big wedding. They are so focused on the excitement of the day, they don't honestly question whether or not they are going to be able to stand living with this man for the rest of their lives.

What are these mistakes?

1. Pretending to be in love just because you've been dating a long time and everyone else thinks you're perfect for each other
2. Not being mature enough or ready to marry, but getting caught up in the romantic fantasy and planning for the wedding
3. Marrying to prove adulthood or because you don't know what else to do with your life
4. Failing to heed the warning signs that the man you are marrying has emotional problems, and trusting that marriage will fix those problems

Girls get caught up in the process and seem helpless to stop it. Imagine you're a girl from a small town, and everyone keeps asking if you have a boyfriend yet. You don't, but you understand there's an expectation that you will find a boyfriend who will turn into a husband. Under pressure, and fearing to take on the world alone, you start dating an old friend because he seems safe and comfortable. Soon you are planning a wedding. It just happens to coincide with graduation and getting that first apartment, which is very convenient, right?

There might be "checks in the spirit." You know, those little niggling doubts you have that you try to suppress that would have warned you that you could be facing deeper problems later on. Perhaps he is a hothead and gets into confrontations a bit too easily, or he borrows money constantly and doesn't pay it back.

But things are moving too fast and that wedding dress is so gorgeous. The bridesmaids have already been chosen. The invitations have been printed. And he looks so handsome in that tux, even though he tells you he hates dressing up in that "monkey suit."

So those uneasy feelings get suppressed. After all, you do really care about this man and everyone would be upset if you stopped things now. Good girl that you are, you just swallow those errant thoughts and keep right on planning.

The years pass by, and eventually you can suppress the feelings no longer. In fact, those little things that bothered you back then now drive you absolutely crazy. You realize that God may have been trying to warn you. But just about the time you think about God, someone comes along at work and shows you a little attention, and the rest is history. Your marriage is busted and your children are brokenhearted. It happens all the time.

You have to be sure God is really calling you to marry someone, and not just go along with it because it is convenient and feels like a safe life choice. You have to grow up before you marry, and that requires accomplishing some very difficult life tasks. It is important that women get their educations, learn how to live without being dependent on a man, and develop an intimate and trusting relationship with God before they throw their lot in with a man. Marrying is not a substitute for becoming a full, whole, functioning person—it either delays your progress or it makes the process much more complicated. Trying to grow up and learning to be married at the same time is a difficult, often painful thing to do. Marriages often tend to grow *apart* when the people within them are trying also to grow *up*.

GEORGIA'S BIG EVENTS

Georgia was a forty-two-year-old woman who came to my office seeking therapy because her husband had left her after almost twenty years of marriage. She was deeply hurt and suffering depression from the abandonment, even though it had been a year since he had moved out and the divorce was now final. She never had a career. Instead, she had devoted herself to helping her husband build his law practice, entertaining, and volunteering in the community.

Georgia became a Christian soon after the birth of her last child and was quite active in a big traditional church in the small southern town where she lived. However, she had quit going to church after her son drowned in a boating accident while they vacationed off the coast of Maine eight years before. The loss of their son caused Georgia to believe God had abandoned her and caused her husband to start drinking heavily. That and Georgia's depression caused the marriage to sour over the years.

When asked to share her life history, Georgia stated that during her adolescence her mother had been controlling and critical, and she felt she had always lacked confidence in herself as a result. She thought she was more like her quiet father, and portrayed herself as a "daddy's girl." Despite her deep insecurity, Georgia developed a reputation as a popular debutante known for always having a good time. Her frequent escort during her coming-out season had been Brad, the son of a socially prominent family friend, on whom she had a big crush.

After drinking too much one evening, Georgia and Brad had sex. Georgia admitted in therapy that she had seduced Brad, hoping sexual intimacy would secure the relationship. But shortly thereafter, Brad broke up with her and the two headed off to separate universities. Georgia pretended to take the rejection nonchalantly, but secretly she was devastated. After the breakup, she was horrified to learn she was pregnant, and without telling anyone, she had an abortion.

In college, Georgia partied a great deal and confessed she had a number of casual sexual encounters, but no serious relationships. She admitted she would fall in love too fast and scare young men off with her emotional intensity. Actually, she was ashamed of herself and deeply wounded by the loss of Brad and her baby. She perceived herself to be a failure and partied frenetically as a way to escape her depression.

YOU CAN'T DISTRACT YOURSELF FOREVER.

In March of her senior year in college, Georgia's father died unexpectedly of a heart attack. The sudden loss of her only supportive parent stunned her, but she surprised everyone by taking off with friends right after the funeral to Key West for spring break. Georgia freely admitted in therapy that the trip was an act of avoidance. She felt her mother had never really loved her father, which had caused a lot of tension and unhappiness during her childhood. Upon returning, Georgia managed to pass her exams and then headed straight to Maine to work as a camp counselor for the summer.

But in mid-July Georgia collapsed in nervous exhaustion. Her doctors sent her back home to her mother to rest. Not understanding the nature of her daughter's problems, she called Georgia's old boyfriend, Brad, who happened to be home for the summer before he started law school in the fall. Georgia had reservations about resuming their relationship, but she was curious to see what would happen. Once again she found herself infatuated with him and, without ever telling him about the abortion, the two soon decided to marry.

Georgia suspected in her heart that she would only be a "trophy wife" for Brad, and she feared deep down that history would repeat itself. But she convinced herself that everything would be fine once they were married and she could get out from underneath her dictatorial, critical mother. In addition, as a nominal Christian, she rationalized that marrying Brad would also provide a way of making up for her abortion, from which she had never healed. She reasoned this would help atone for her past mistakes. They would have children and live a good life. She would be the best mother possible. She could forget the past once and for all.

Little did she know that the foundation she was laying for her life was full of cracks. For twenty years Georgia had planned enough Big Events to last a lifetime in an attempt to cover the potholes in her soul. The death of her son had brought her to the end of that journey. With no more events to plan and no more pretense of spirituality, Georgia was broken.

WE ARE SO BUSY WONDERING IF WE FIT IN THAT WE CAN'T TRULY ENJOY THE PRESENCE OF GOD.

You don't have to experience the death of a child, an abortion, or a major life event to fall into the habit of staging events to avoid essential life tasks. Women all over avoid completing important life tasks by marrying and having children, building houses, and getting bigger jobs. They move from one big purchase to the next, and when they get a good job, they set their eyes immediately on getting their supervisor's job. They buy a car, only to upgrade when a friend gets a better car and they decide they have to keep up. They move frequently to bigger and better homes or constantly remodel the ones they have. They keep seeking "something more," hoping to distract themselves from having to examine their lives too closely.

The problem is, you can't distract yourself forever, nor can you fill your emptiness with "things."

SPIRITUALIZED NARCISSISM

GOD WANTS

YOU TO HAVE

"ABUNDANT LIFE."

Often, when the yearning for something more becomes intense, that's when women will turn to church.

If a woman is motivated to go to church because she wants salvation and new birth, then that is absolutely the right place to turn. But too often, women join a church with no intention of admitting their needs to another person. Fearful of what others might think if they admitted their shame, discontent, petty jealousies, and secret yearnings, these women don a mask when they enter the doors. They may look the part and say the right things—that they "want more of God"—but in actuality, what they're really after is more of the good things they hope God is handing out.

It's not uncommon for women to compare themselves to other women in church. We wonder if we dress well enough or if others think we appear smart or good enough to be in their social circle. We get our feelings hurt by some imagined snub or inferred remark. We are so busy wondering if we fit in that we can't truly enjoy the presence of God, especially if we overhear someone talking about a social event we weren't included in.

I know some of you are in difficult situations, and often the joy you get from participating in social events allows you to survive. Perhaps you are in a horrible marriage that you cannot end or you are dealing with terminal illness or grief over the loss of a loved one or a prodigal child.

I've had many painful losses in my life, and there were times when a good Wednesday night supper or looking forward to a wedding or a party helped me survive those terrible times. I thank God for those simple comforts and distractions. There is nothing wrong with taking emotional comfort from social events, if doing so is kept in perspective.

I'm not talking about comforting yourself in healthy ways in the midst of situations you cannot change. I am, however, challenging you to examine how you manage to avoid doing important internal work by focusing on external events that distract you from that process, and how this leads to depression, boredom, emptiness, and craving for something more. Because you don't have the discipline and understanding to sit at the feet of Jesus and turn your yearnings toward him, you get drawn into the world and all its meaningless distractions.

FINDING SOMETHING MORE

Christ wants you to get to the root of your yearnings. He wants to give you a sense of fullness and satisfaction that comes from placing your energies into the work he has called you to do, not in staging one meaningless event after the other. If the *something more* you long for is more of Christ, start praying to him. Really talk to him. But if you avoid prayer, don't offer true service helping those who are worse off than you, and fail to examine your life in light of the gospel, then you are addicted to the things of the world, and that is what will get you in trouble.

God wants you to have "abundant life"—not just a life that is in the doldrums without a big, exciting something on the horizon. Besides, it is hard to develop a "servant spirit" if you are focused on a "ta-da" experience all the time.

After all, God is the Big Event that should be happening to you on a daily basis, and trust me, there won't be fireworks every day. In fact, if you are living in his will, there's a good possibility you'll be doing a lot of menial tasks that aren't glamorous or fun at all.

A wonderful book, *The Sacred Romance* by John Eldredge and Brent Curtis (Nelson, 1997), describes the kind of excitement and Big Events God wants for our lives. God does want us to live a Big Life. But if, as women, we focus on the external distractions, we will never get that kind of largeness of life that God intends.

Do you know why I started shopping in thrift shops? At first it started out of necessity, because I didn't have the money then and I like nice things. But even though I can now afford nicer things, I no longer want them. God used that time of financial stress to teach me important principles of thrift, stewardship, and priority-setting. I realized I had the money to spend on writing conferences, educational travel, and good computer software instead of dresses, accessories, and entertainment. I realized that living from one social event to another wasn't going to make my dreams of having a significant life come true. In fact, now I rarely spend money on Christmas presents or holiday festivities either. I collect one-of-a-kind presents I find in flea markets or tag sales, and I decorate with live greenery or a tiny tree. I rarely go on big vacations that aren't educational in nature. I don't entertain unless it is to have a few friends or family over for a casual meal.

I want the time and effort I expend to mean something. I want my efforts to be significant in God's eyes. I don't want to wake up the morning after a big party wondering why I wasted my precious energies on planning a social occasion that did nothing to further the kingdom of God.

There is going to be a huge wedding feast when Christ returns. If you want a fulfilled life, that's the only Big Event you really need to plan for.

PART TWO

TRAPPED IN THE
MAGIC MIRROR

CHAPTER FIVE

THE POISON
IN THE APPLE

Your desire shall be for your husband,
and he shall rule over you.

—Genesis 3:16

$\mathcal{D}$o you remember what it felt like the first time you ever felt ashamed of yourself for something you did as a child? Do you remember that first sickening realization that you had the ability to be disobedient—that you could steal, look at dirty pictures you found in an old *Playboy* magazine, or deliberately tell a secret someone had told you not to tell?

I have a vivid memory of the first time I did something that made me ashamed of myself. The memory still has the power to make me sad if I happen to think about it on one of those days when the Accuser is trying to beat me to a pulp.

It happened when I was about seven years old. I was

attending a very small rural school and there was only one other little girl in my class, so for the most part I played with little boys. I was the oldest child in my family and didn't have any brothers at the time, and my dad treated me very much like the little boy he had originally wanted. I acted like a tomboy, even though my mother, bless her heart, would try without success to keep my skinned knees and mosquito bites covered up with frilly dresses.

My friends, Steve and William, were my constant companions. We all lived just a few miles from each other in the country. In general, the world seemed a safe place for children back then, so we rambled a lot in the woods and played in nearby barns and haylofts. Occasionally, one of us would have to stop to go to the bathroom, and of course, after a while, that got our curiosity stirred up. I don't remember exactly the first time Steve and I decided to look at each other and see for ourselves what our differences were, but I remember quite well the way my heart hammered and my mouth became dry when we did. I knew something was wrong about what we were doing.

If we could look at each other without shame, why were we wearing clothes and why were our parents always telling us not to touch ourselves "down there"? Why did Steve get such a sly look on his face when he unzipped his pants to pee? Even as a child, I figured out there was more to the whole subject than anyone was telling us. Perhaps it was the fact that no one would talk about it that made me feel as if what I was doing was wrong. If anything, that sneaky feeling just made the game more exciting. William, Steve, and I played "doctor and nurse" all the time and healed more broken bones and gave more shots in hind parts than we'll ever experience in real life. But it wasn't my parents who really shamed me. Another child did.

One day, during recess, a classmate ran up to me, grinning horribly. Alvin grabbed me with his dirty hands, kissed me roughly on the cheek, and ran off laughing with maniacal glee. I can feel his slobbery lips and spittle even now.

Running, he pointed back at me, shouting loudly enough for everyone to hear, "Steve told me what you do with him in the barn!"

My heart froze. I'm sure I looked like Bambi caught in headlights. I could have easily died of shame right at that very moment. But I pretended not to hear him and kept my shameful secret to myself. For weeks I had nightmares about being in a circle of children who taunted me until I ran off crying.

THE MORE OF THAT APPLE WE EAT, THE MORE WE SEEM TO CRAVE.

Most children engage in sexual play in childhood at some point. If you have children and are concerned about this kind of behavior, please remember that shaming tactics are not healthy ways to control the problem.[††]

I was devastated, and until now I don't think I've ever told anyone about it.

Of course, Steve and I weren't friends after that, even though we were forced to play together many times until his family moved away. But I never felt the same way about him because he had betrayed our friendship. More important, I never felt the same way about myself ever again.

I had taken my first little nibble on the apple of shame.

Wouldn't it be wonderful if that first bite would inoculate us for life and we would know once and for all the difference

---

[††] I've cited a resource in the back of the book to answer your questions.

between good and evil—and that knowledge would save us forever from the heartache and pain that comes when we disobey God?

But you and I both know it doesn't. In fact, most of the time the opposite happens. The more of that apple we eat, the more we seem to crave. The more we crave, the more we eat—and after a while, we are so full of the poison of shame and self-doubt, we don't care anymore. That's who we are and there seems to be no going back.

Pretty soon we've eaten the whole apple, worms and all.

INNOCENCE LOST

All of us have read the story of "Snow White and the Seven Dwarfs," and most of us have probably seen the movie a hundred times. We know it as well as

THE LITTLE GIRL

DIDN'T KNOW THAT

WAS A LIE.

we know most Bible stories. Of course, everyone loves the darling Snow White, the victim of all victims, who lies in a glass bubble while seven little people cry for her loss. And, like most fairy tales, she lives happily ever after once she is kissed by the prince.

Don't you realize there is a reason we call them "fairy" tales?

If you read the story carefully, I believe the character that we need to examine more closely in this chapter is the queen, because it was the queen who was trapped in the Magic Mirror, and that is the subject of this book. We won't ever truly understand how easy it is to get trapped until we understand how much of the queen resides in each of us.

So, with that in mind, let's look at a portrait of the queen.

But the new Queen hated Snow White. She was jealous of the young princess's beauty and feared that
one day Snow White would be considered the most
beautiful in the kingdom. That is why every day she
would ask her magic mirror, "Mirror, mirror on the
wall, who is the fairest one of all?" And as long as the
mirror would reply, "You are," the Queen was
happy. But one day, a handsome Prince pronounced
that he was in love with Snow White, even though
she was not royalty. The Queen was furious and
afraid that her worst fears had come true. When she
demanded that her mirror tell her the truth, it
replied, "Snow White is fairer than thee." In her
rage, the Queen ordered her guards to kill the
princess and bring her heart back in a small box.
(paraphrased from the original folktale "Little Snow
White")

THE QUEEN WAS ONCE A CHILD

Can you imagine the queen as a small child? She might not
have been too different from you and me before she started
talking to that mirror. But somewhere along the way she
became horribly insecure and fearful. Perhaps she was sexually
abused, was very overweight, or suffered a tragedy early in life.
Perhaps she simply had parents who criticized and shamed her
all the time.

In order to suppress her self-doubt and fear of the future, she
started staring into her mirror, and lo and behold, there was
somebody in the mirror staring back. And that somebody
seemed to speak for everybody, so she started asking it questions.
It told her that it was the Magic Mirror and that it would help
her be strong and powerful. It told her that she could be beautiful, get everything she wanted, and … live happily ever after.

But the little girl didn't know that was a lie.

I am not saying that we should feel sorry for the queen. The adult queen was a terrible, evil woman. But most women, even those who are queens, don't start out that way. In fact, most start out as an innocent child, just like Snow White.

Just like us.

In my practice I counsel children as well as adults. Frequently, a child—most often a girl—will come to see me because of depression and social anxiety issues. Obsessed with her self-image, body shape, weight, and height, she is sad and angry. Many hate the way they look and who they are, and often admit they secretly despise other children who they believe "have it all."

THE DRIVE FOR

PERFECTION IS

SPIRALING WAY

OUT OF CONTROL.

By most standards, these children are normal. But that's exactly what they cannot bear. They can't stand the thought that they might be normal or ordinary. They long to stand out above all the others. They think they are losers because they are just normal.

Over time, most admit that they have secrets. The secrets are not always dramatic. Sometimes they are as simple as having played "doctor" with a sibling or friend or even having wished that their baby sister or brother would die so they could get all the attention.

Other times the secrets are terrible. Their parents may have damaged them emotionally by telling them repeatedly that they are bad, they may have been molested by a parent or family member, or they may have been abandoned. Some are afraid their parents might divorce, and some know secrets about their parents' affairs or substance abuse.

But sometimes there is no dramatic secret; they have just been overindulged by their parents. They believe they are entitled to special treatment, and as a result of not getting it, they feel jealousy and malice towards others.

The common theme is that they share an inner belief that they are defective in some manner and that bad things are going to happen to them because of it. Terrified someone is going to find out what they are really like on the inside, they often think they would rather die than live with the shame of exposure.

Unless they commit their lives to Christ and are mentored by a mature Christian in adulthood, many will always be dissatisfied with themselves regardless of what they achieve in life. No matter how much plastic surgery, weight loss, speech training, or eye correction they have in the future, they will continue to be unhappy with themselves. Regardless of how much money they eventually make or how many awards they win, they have ingested the poison of shame, and eventually it will infiltrate their entire lives.

THE ETERNAL QUEST

Many will become queens. They will seek validation from the Magic Mirror. They will become obsessed with being beautiful, rich, and sexy. Here are some sobering facts to support my claims:

- Five to ten million women and girls suffer from anorexia and/or bulimia in the U.S. (This is a general estimate—the behavior is often kept secret and therefore difficult to quantify.)
- In 2003, 5,606 people age eighteen and under received Botox injections. Between 2000 and 2004 there was a 244 percent increase in Botox injections.

- Breast implants for women have increased almost 1000 percent in the last ten years.
- Between 2000 and 2004 there was a 29 percent increase in liposuction and a 75 percent increase in nose reshaping.
- Breast implants for girls eighteen and younger increased 300 percent from 2002 to 2003. (All statistics are from the American Society of Plastic Surgeons Web site.)

The drive for perfection is spiraling way out of control, and our children are the ultimate victims.

THE QUEEN AS A METAPHOR

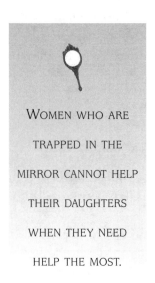

WOMEN WHO ARE TRAPPED IN THE MIRROR CANNOT HELP THEIR DAUGHTERS WHEN THEY NEED HELP THE MOST.

Yes, the queen is an embodiment of all the females in our lives who have hurt us, and a powerful force in the world today. But the queen is more than that.

The queen lives in all of us.

If that weren't the case, we could just blame our mothers and all those other women who hurt us for all of our problems, and justify our own mistakes by saying that "the queen made me do it."

But that would be a form of denial. To demonize the queen is to put the blame on something or someone other than ourselves. Like blaming Satan, it can become an excuse for poor decision making on our own parts. It allows us to distance ourselves from the evil queen, feel righteous about ourselves, and believe that we are victims like poor Snow White. The end result is that we perpetuate the myth that if we are just "good enough" then bad things won't happen to us, we control our lives, and thus we will live happily ever after.

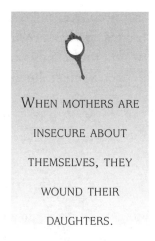

WHEN MOTHERS ARE INSECURE ABOUT THEMSELVES, THEY WOUND THEIR DAUGHTERS.

The truth is that just because we have given our lives to Christ and we are trying hard to live a Christlike life doesn't mean we have overcome the queen inside or that we will live a life that has a fairy-tale ending. Yes, it is true that when we are saved we are "new creatures in Christ." But the battle is not over just because we give our lives to Christ.

Every Queen starts as a Snow White, and the truth is that we've all taken a bite of the apple at some point in our lives. Some of us got over it, some of us fell asleep, and some of us are still flirting with that mirror.

MANY KINDS OF QUEENS

The queen comes from without as well. She may come as a critical mother, the woman in church who snubs you, or the teenage daughter who tells you she hates you. Whoever she is, it is her presence that has made it difficult for women to trust each other. Women who trust are women who get hurt, plain and simple. If we hurt deeply enough, we learn not to love or to trust at all. If we hurt long enough, we may turn into queens ourselves. Women don't seem to trust each other at all sometimes. We compete so hard to be the *most* attractive, the *best* dressed, and the one who gets the *most* attention that we sacrifice friendships with other women. We avoid making friends, or we become so defensive and self-protective we wound the friends we have without realizing it.

Yet, women should be our most valuable allies. Whether in the wars of the spirit or just in the battles of everyday life, women need to stick together. Chapter 11 is devoted to the topic of how to make the kinds of friends who last for a lifetime.

WHEN THE QUEEN IS A MOTHER

But what if the women who hurt us are our mothers? And what if we are mothers who have hurt our daughters?

There is an insidious factor ruining mother/daughter relationships these days. Many mothers are not adequately parenting their daughters because they are too focused on their own insecurities and romantic addictions. Women who are trapped in the mirror cannot help their daughters when they need help the most, or teach their daughters how to form positive relationships with other females.

The competition for being the "fairest of them all" in the household can result in conflict in the mother/daughter relationship as well, in the form of jealousy, power struggles, and feelings of anger and abandonment on both sides.

Men may have the power to make us feel physically attractive, but women have the ability to make us feel strong, spiritually powerful, and beautiful on the inside. But when mothers are insecure about themselves, they wound their daughters, and thus insecurity is passed on to their daughters.

All mothers make mistakes. All daughters make mistakes. In the process we wound each other. Unfortunately, it is often because we love our daughters so much that we inadvertently wound them the deepest. And this is what our daughters may pass on to their daughters as well if they do not understand how to break the cycle.

- Women overreact when their daughters make mistakes (particularly sexual) and intensify their daughters' feelings of shame and inadequacy. This is common among those trying to raise Christian daughters. We fear our daughters inherited our tendencies toward disobedience and immorality and will repeat our mistakes. Our shame and guilt become reflected in the shame and guilt of our daughters.
- We hide our own mistakes and failures and the wounds we suffered as young girls. We cannot honestly discuss our own sexual mistakes as young women—and the pain they brought us—with our daughters. Thus, they feel too ashamed to discuss their mistakes with us.
- We put too much emphasis on our daughters' physical beauty and support those activities that make us look good as parents rather than on those that challenge her to be strong and individualistic.

THE MIRROR CAN

ULTIMATELY

BECOME FATAL.

- Though meaning well, we become manipulative of social situations so our daughters will be popular and not suffer the pain of exclusion like we did. This shames our daughters instead of empowering them, because these actions infer we don't have faith in their abilities to handle their own social lives.

- We encourage our daughters' friendships or participation in programs or activities that promote narcissism and unhealthy competition with other girls. Cheerleading, beauty pageants, and clubs can be lethal if led by leaders who promote wrong values in the group.
- We compete with other women, and we model that for our daughters.
- Because we are insecure, we cover our feelings by gossiping, criticizing, or constantly finding fault with other women.
- We spend too much on clothing and entertainment for both our daughters and ourselves.
- We insist on perfection in everything we do.
- We cannot bear to be seen without makeup, obsess about how much we weigh, and secretly enjoy it when we know other women are intimidated by our style, achievements, or material possessions.
- We suffer depression, anger, and unhappiness when we don't get the attention and praise from others we crave, which causes our families to resent our continual need for affirmation from them.
- We do not respect ourselves, take care of our bodies, or exhibit a healthy self-value. Instead, we become "martyrs to motherhood."
- We need to be the center of attention in every situation.
- We allow ourselves to be abused physically, emotionally, or verbally by husbands and boyfriends. Our daughters then allow men to do the same to them.
- We do not set loving limits and are inconsistent in our parenting.

- We discuss our marriage or relationship problems with our children and treat them as best friends and confidantes instead of the children they are. We form codependent relationships with our daughters, using them as our therapists and undermining their growth toward independence and maturity.
- We encourage our daughters' unhealthy dependence upon us. We do not help them share their painful secrets, or recognize their need for help when they are in emotional trouble. We teach them to pretend and "act nice" regardless of how sad or frightened they really are.
- We discuss our children with others in negative ways in their presence.
- We criticize their appearance and tell them they need to lose weight.
- We do not spend enough time on our own spiritual growth and development.
- We are not happy with ourselves, so therefore our daughters don't want to be anything like us.

WHEN THE MIRROR BECOMES FATAL

If taken to its worst conclusion, we all know the mirror can ultimately become fatal. It certainly was for the queen. Let's go back and look a bit closer at how the story of Snow White ends.

> All seven of them rushed to save their beloved Snow White, but it was too late. They spotted the queen and ran after her. As she was trying to escape, she slipped off a cliff and plummeted to her doom. (Disney version)

I don't think it is an accident that the names of the seven little weird guys chasing the queen are those names assigned to emotions, physical states, or the medical treatment associated with mood disorders: Happy, Sleepy, Sneezy, Grumpy, Dopey, Bashful, and Doc.

Snow White simply fell asleep. But the queen was chased off a cliff and plummeted to her death. Sad that she became an old hag and that emotions killed her in the end. That is what happens when you talk to a mirror.

CHAPTER SIX

A HOUSE OF MIRRORS

Take heed that no one deceives you.

—Matthew 24:4

The last time I looked in a three-way mirror in a department store, I got a rude awakening. Talk about reality therapy! I could no longer pretend I didn't need to get to the gym as quickly as possible. It is amazing how easy it is to trick yourself into believing you look just fine when all you see is the front view of yourself. But three views, and from all angles? No way.

If a three-way mirror is that bad, can you imagine what it's like to visit a house of mirrors?

I stay as far away from them as I can, because the thought of getting trapped by multiple images of myself frightens me terribly.

These days, growing up as an American teen is like navigating a house of mirrors—it's confusing, scary, disorienting, and misleading. With so many potential selves to choose from and false doors beckoning, there are just too many opportunities to choose dead-end roads.

Some of you may have lingering confusion and unhealed wounds from your early years that continue to drive your behavior. You cannot decide which of the messages you absorbed are truth and which are lies. Just like in adolescence, you are still wandering around the house of mirrors dazed and disoriented.

HOW ADOLESCENTS BECOME CONFUSED

The church is full of people who are emotionally unstable. They are people who have been wounded by life, and the church is exactly where they should be. Many of them struggle financially, experience marital problems, and never learned how to parent children in a positive way because they did not have positive role models. This may be one of the reasons why they feel attracted to religion, and specifically to church, because church offers the family feeling of stability and safety they rarely experienced growing up.

But more often they take the negative communication patterns they have learned as children into their relationships in church. Not only do they hurt others, but they become wounded themselves, often in the very place where they sought solace and community. They experience the same secretive, closed communication patterns in church as they experienced growing up in their families and are wounded all over again in the very place they thought they were going to enjoy love and acceptance.

This confuses our children. And in the process, they learn secrecy, manipulation, power struggle, and hypocrisy in ways we, as parents, never planned.

In my own situation, my children witnessed that type of behavior in several different churches we attended and assumed Christians were hypocritical and the Christian faith didn't work. It saddens me to say that to a large degree they have not yet recovered from some of the wounds they suffered.

THE MOST DESTRUCTIVE FORM OF DECEPTION IS THAT WHICH IS WITHIN.

My children additionally found it difficult to reconcile their conflicting desires to please their Christian parents *and* to fit in with their peer group, most of whom were themselves living in Christian homes. However, I've learned through the years that many of the friends they had that I thought were positive Christian role models were not actually living out their beliefs in their private lives. This can be very confusing for children as well. They assume everyone is just as deceptive as they are.

THE AGE OF DECEPTION

Ever since the birth of the information age, deception has been the ruling spirit of our world. Because of that, it's more difficult than ever for children to follow what seems to be the simplistic faith of their parents.

In fact, Jesus tells us quite plainly in Matthew 24:10–13 that in these latter days, "many will be offended, will betray one another, and will hate one another.... many false prophets will rise up and deceive many. And because lawlessness will abound, the love of many will grow cold. But he who endures to the end shall be saved."

Thank God for the last sentence of that passage.

I don't think young people today have a more difficult time in general than other adolescents have had in other periods of history—the problems are just different. Particularly in America, our affluence has created a whole new set of problems for certain groups simply because life has become far too easy for many, at least financially.

Many teenagers today spend as much money on their music as their grandparents earned in a whole year. Poor kids who cannot afford MP3s, $150 shoes, and name-brand clothing suffer a sense of despair and anger because they see the results of affluence around them all the time. And we wonder why they resort to violence and selling drugs.

The world has always been a scary place. The weapons have just gotten to be a bit more sophisticated and accessible. The difference now, however, is that we no longer know who really has them or who the enemy really is. The guy sitting next to us in the pew at church could be a serial killer. The very leaders we have appointed to protect and keep us safe deceive us, no matter which particular party line they espouse. The media deceives us in order to gain our advertising dollars. Issues like marriage, family, politics, and gender identity have all been clouded because evil is disguised as goodness and light—something I believe hasn't been quite as true in the past as in the current age.

The most destructive form of deception, however, is that which is within. We shadowbox with reality and illusion. What makes things so different now is that our children see deception on the media on a daily basis. A commercial is airing on television this year that I absolutely despise. It shows a teenage boy in the car with his dad swearing on his life that he did not drive his father's car, but when his dad cranks the engine, rock music blares out.

What message does that send? It teaches that deception is a natural part of being a teenager, and the better you are at it, the happier you will be.

In this postmodern age, everything is up for grabs. Mark Tabb, in *Mission to Oz* (Moody Press, 2004, 37–38), writes the following:

> The postmodern ... tolerates every idea of right and wrong, truth and lie, normal and abnormal, only because it does not believe any one absolute standard exists. And if one absolute standard does not exist, every other standard is equally true, because they are all equally false. All are nothing more than man-made illusion with no basis in fact. Deep down, people in this land are convinced that nothing is real, nothing is true, and nothing matters. Even so, they embrace everything, behaving as though their personal preferences of truth validate themselves.

Like me, Tabb credits much of the "man-made illusion" to the pseudorealities we've been exposed to via television and marketing. Because nothing is real, there is really no such thing as a lie. If everything is about personal preference and truth is relative, then children have no reason not to deceive their parents, because after all, who knows if parents are being truthful and honest themselves?

Scripture predicted this problem: "For men will be ... disobedient to parents ... having a form of godliness, but denying its power" (2 Tim. 3:2–5).

In other words, the duality of this present age was actually prophesied in the book of Timothy. In the latter days young men and women would disobey their parents and defy the teachings of the church. They would pretend to be religious while denying their faith had any value or power in their lives.

Without a doubt, the media has presented our children with an alternative reality and caused many to turn from their faith. But they don't own all the blame.

ADOLESCENTS AND HYPOCRISY

In homes where great importance was placed on maintaining a successful appearance, some children were fed a hypocritical message about Christianity. Their parents told them to follow Christ, but spent all their time and emotional energy on making money and getting ahead in the world—to the exclusion of following and modeling the teachings of Christ.

MANY TEENS FEEL CAUGHT IN A DOUBLE BIND.

The message these children internalized is that we must follow Christ, but not if we end up looking like failures, not if we don't have a cute boyfriend, and not if it means we don't go to college. And for young women, there was an added disclaimer: not if it meant marrying a man too poor to provide all the accoutrements of worldly success.

I've worked with hundreds of teenagers through the years as a social worker, teacher, and director of Christian education in addition to my counseling. What I've observed is that, like their parents, many teens feel caught in a double bind. They are attempting to be Christians, but are having great trouble saying no to the pressures put on them by their peers to become sexually active or to be successful by worldly standards. I believe this pressure is intensified when parents send the subtle message that their child must have it all. Parents are in denial about the realities of life for their teens, especially their daughters. The truth is that it is almost impossible for purity and popularity to coexist these days, no matter how badly parents may want to believe otherwise.

This deeply concerns me. I fear for the future of the young men and women who will one day have to reap the whirlwind of casual sexuality and the pursuit of materialism. But I also fear for the parents who send the message to their children that following the teachings of Christ is to be taken seriously only as long as it doesn't interfere with getting rich or being popular. Jesus said those who cause children to stumble would be better off being drowned! (See Matt. 18:6.)

WE BECOME USED TO PRETENDING THAT WE COME FROM PERFECT FAMILIES.

The truth is that if you are *really* following Christ, you are going to suffer rejection, ridicule, and unpopularity. This is called "spiritual warfare." And people are probably going to think you are weird as well.

I know few people who understand how true this is. To follow Christ is to experience pain and possible rejection. That is a very, very hard truth to accept.

HIDDEN PROBLEMS IN THE CHRISTIAN HOME

Many of us grew up in homes where there was a lot of substance abuse and addiction. Homes like this are filled with what counselors call "toxic secrets," those shameful things that have happened but that no one talks about. Those are the "elephants in the living room"—a term made popular in the Adult Children of Alcoholics literature—that no one admits are actually there.

We hear the elephant, smell the elephant, and clean up the elephant's poop, but we pretend that there is no elephant. There are big secrets about something that everyone is pretending didn't happen, such as Mama's addiction to pain pills, Daddy's womanizing, or Grandpa's getting drunk and hitting Grandma all the time.

These are things no one will talk about because they are too ashamed. But you'd never know a thing was wrong, looking in from the outside. Everybody looks good, acts nice, and appears successful—at least when out in public.

Children in homes like these learn to be good actors at a very young age. All emotional energy is concentrated on keeping up the appearance of normalcy. This generates from the false belief that if something bad is happening in their family, it must be because they are bad people. This produces a deep sense of shame and guilt. Secrecy and denial are the result, which leads to a greater sense of shame.

Good Christian families never have these kinds of problems, right?

Of course they do. In fact, most families have problems. But if no one in the family talks about the problems when we are children, we become used to pretending that we come from perfect families. Deep inside we are horribly ashamed of who we are; then we act out that shame in our own lives. We repeat the family history of which we are so ashamed!

That is why it is so important to discuss family history with your children and not keep the secrets buried. Discuss them openly, honestly, and compassionately, and model forgiveness and understanding for your children. Trust me, if you don't tell your children about the problems, they will hear about them from someone else anyway, and it will be twice as painful. Of course, you should wait until they are old enough, leave out unnecessary painful details, and use discretion when you do.

Don't wound your children by telling them things that should be forgotten or that are no longer relevant, either. Stick to telling only about those things that may be impacting you and your children in a negative way in the present.

My purpose in all of this is to help you think about your childhood and your family history. Are there painful family secrets that are still having an effect on the present? I want you to think about some of the experiences you may have suffered growing up because you were living a dual existence. Are you carrying toxic secrets, and are you bringing some of the resulting guilt and shame from those events into your life and marriage now?

Living a Lie

Melanie and Tom came to me for marital counseling due to her severe depression and their marital unhappiness. Both were in their early thirties, and the marriage was in high conflict, with little sexual contact or emotional intimacy between the couple. Melanie claimed Tom was obsessed with his work, spent little time with her, and was often too tired for lovemaking. Melanie hungered for emotional intimacy. She admitted she felt lonely and abandoned by her husband.

Melanie and Tom had been high school sweethearts, both reared in strict Christian homes. Though Tom grew up in a traditional home with emotionally healthy parents, Melanie's father had abandoned both Melanie and her mother when she was a young child and had never contacted them again. Her mother struggled to raise a child on her own. Melanie harbored secret fears that her birth had been the catalyst for her father's abandonment of the family.

She admitted that, as a result, she had been a sad, angry adolescent and had acted out by becoming promiscuous in high school. But she pretended to be a "good girl" who attended youth group regularly and sang in the church choir. Melanie's mother placed a high value on the appearance that everything was "just fine." She made sure Melanie was well dressed and had all the advantages other kids had, sometimes to the point where they could barely meet expenses because her mother felt that having nice clothes and keeping up appearances was so important.

Melanie's mother would often fly into hysterical rages when she was overstressed or tired, and would suffer migraines for days on end. Melanie claimed her mother was always looking for a husband, and unfortunately, had an affair with a married supervisor at the company where she worked. Melanie overheard a great deal during the affair and noticed her mother's eyes were swollen and red after heated phone conversations. As a result, she worried about her mother, their finances, and their future, and felt deeply ashamed of what she imagined might be going on in her mother's life.

Melanie wanted to talk with her mother about those things, but she considered her mother to be too emotionally fragile to deal with them. Like her mother, she resorted to pretending that everything was just fine at home and in church, but she acted out her feelings in self-destructive ways by dating "bad boys" who always left her feeling abandoned. On numbers of occasions, she became frightened by some of her sexual experiences and feared she would end up like her mother.

When she met Tom, she was relieved to find someone who gave her life structure and meaning. Because he did not push her to have sex and was often very parental with her, she found herself clinging to him for the safety and security she had never had. He was active in church and a good student. Even more important, his family was very traditional, without the major scandals or secrets that had dominated Melanie's life.

While they dated, Melanie attended a local community college for a two-year degree, though she admitted she struggled with depression throughout her time there. She had always dreamed of going to a major university and leaving her small town forever.

MELANIE WAS
TRAPPED IN THE
MAGIC MIRROR.

During this time, Melanie noticed that Tom wasn't showing her a lot of attention and became irritated at her attempts to show him affection. But she had been impressed with his devout faith and his insistence that God had brought them together—and with the fact that he seemed to be headed toward a promising career.

The couple married upon Tom's graduation from college, and because he wanted children so badly, Melanie quickly became pregnant. When that child was two, the doctors informed Melanie that she had endometriosis and she and Tom should go ahead and have another baby soon if they wanted more children. Even though she felt uneasy and was already suffering depression and dissatisfaction with Tom's long work hours and lack of intimacy, she agreed to another pregnancy.

When they began counseling, Melanie was suffering severe postpartum depression and said that she hated staying at home during the day with the couple's two young children. In addition, the last baby had been a colicky baby and a poor sleeper. Tom was in pharmaceutical sales and traveled much of the week. He felt Melanie was being disobedient to God and should be happy with her home and children. However, Melanie wanted to continue her education and create a career for herself, fearing that if her marriage failed she would have no means of support. Tom insisted that this would not happen and was angry at the thought of Melanie's going to work.

Though Tom professed to love Melanie very much, he admitted he really had always been somewhat irritated by her constant demands for attention, and he was disappointed that she could not enjoy being a stay-at-home mom now. He also claimed that Melanie loved spending money on clothes and entertainment, and though he had a good income that would allow her to stay at home, he was angry because they could not seem to save money for a bigger house for their family. As a young man trying to build his career, Tom felt that he had to work long hours to keep her in the style to which she was accustomed. Tom also confessed that he'd always had a low sex drive and there had never been much affection shown by his parents, so intimacy was not a high priority.

Melanie was an extraordinarily beautiful young woman who revealed she was often the focus of a great deal of male attention while out in public. Though she said she loved Tom, she admitted she struggled with being attracted to other men who were more attentive. She fantasized a great deal about meeting someone more romantic. Melanie had become a fitness junkie and sported a deep tan, perfect hair and nails, and dealt with her depression and boredom with shopping sprees and lunches with girlfriends. She continued to be active in the church, but most of her involvement centered around the social functions (cookouts, retreats, and sports) sponsored by the church.

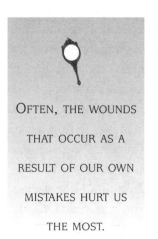

OFTEN, THE WOUNDS THAT OCCUR AS A RESULT OF OUR OWN MISTAKES HURT US THE MOST.

Melanie longed to be a "real" Christian and believed herself to be spiritual, but she questioned if she had the emotional energy anymore to wait for the kind of relationship she had wanted with Tom. In her words, "I want to make the right decisions, but I'm sick of being lonely and never feeling as if I am loved and cherished. When I married Tom, it was because he made me feel safe. Now I just feel trapped. I don't even know anymore how I feel about him, or if I ever loved him at all."

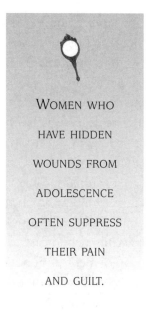

WOMEN WHO HAVE HIDDEN WOUNDS FROM ADOLESCENCE OFTEN SUPPRESS THEIR PAIN AND GUILT.

Melanie began the process of learning that she had justified in her mind at a fairly young age that she had the right to act out her anger and feelings of rejection by her father by having inappropriate sexual encounters while in high school. She had also rationalized that she couldn't tell her mother because of her mother's fragility, when in truth, she was afraid that her mother would become even stricter and she would lose much of the freedom she had earned by having her mother's trust.

But these poor choices had only served to confirm her deep feelings of worthlessness. These—not the abandonment by her father—were the root causes of her depression and her unusual need for constant attention and romance from her husband. They also helped her to rationalize compulsive shopping when Tom was out of town. She realized, too, that no one had prevented her from seeking a career, and that Tom had never pushed her into marriage.

Melanie was trapped in the Magic Mirror.

We began the difficult process of resurrecting the pain of her father's abandonment, her shame-based approach to life, and her deep sense of financial insecurity and low self-worth. Melanie began to understand that her obsession with her appearance and her resultant depression stemmed largely from her lack of confidence in her worth as a woman.

She then was shown that by choosing a man who was cold and withdrawn, she was reenacting the feelings of abandonment she had suffered as a child. When Tom realized the effect his behavior was having on Melanie, he began to work harder at being more emotionally available and less withholding of affection.

Eventually, Melanie did enroll in college to pursue a degree in psychology. She began medication for her depression, which improved her outlook considerably. Tom agreed to pay for part-time child care as long as Melanie did not accept full-time employment until both children were in school. He also agreed to be more supportive of her personal growth as a woman. The two started going out on weekly dates with each other on Saturday evenings and took turns babysitting one night of the week so the other could attend Bible study.

Melanie still struggles with a need for attention and a lack of self-confidence, but she now realizes she needs to work more at finding that from her relationship with God, not exclusively from her husband.

OLD WOUNDS ALWAYS RESURFACE

Believe it or not, Melanie's story is one I encounter frequently. I used it so you could see in a graphic manner how a mind-set is started at an early age because of an original wound. But long after the original wound has lost its importance (in Melanie's case her abandonment by her father), we can still act out our pain because at some point we begin to re-wound ourselves by our own reactionary behavior. Often, the wounds that occur as a result of our own mistakes hurt us the most. It is one thing to be a victim, it is worse to have acted as our own enemy.

These are the abortions we had, the times we got drunk and acted shamefully, or the times we got angry over some loss or hurt experienced at the hand of a parent, then acted it out by smoking pot and having casual sex in the backseat of a car. These actions we now regret have created hidden wounds and firmly planted feelings and beliefs of self-doubt that send us running to the Magic Mirror.

It is these hidden wounds that often drive women into marriages that are difficult. In some cases, women with hidden wounds marry men who are controlling, cold, abusive, or emotionally unavailable, because, like Melanie, these women are looking for a man who will counterbalance the natures they feel are out of control in themselves. Some marry abusive men and tolerate the abuse because they do not value themselves enough to hold out for a man who will treat them well. They reopen the old wound of emotional abandonment and rejection, and play the same theme over and over in their lives. They choose a man who confirms their deepest fears about themselves—that they are not worth being loved like God intended.

Other women with hidden wounds become prodigals. They marry men who enable them to run from their pasts, their parents, and their deep sense of shame, but what they run into is a brick wall of their own making. Too often, these very men will wound them all over again and convince them once and for all that they are not even lovable. Instead of confronting their hidden wounds, both men and women just repeat the same patterns in new relationships that fail, because the old wounds are still festering underneath.

Women who have hidden wounds from adolescence often suppress their pain and guilt in a variety of self-destructive ways. Usually they are excessively controlling, and possibly obsessive about cleanliness, order, and clothing, while their children are expected to behave perfectly at all times. Many become anorexic. Others become compulsive shoppers, and their credit card debt is through the roof, often leading to bankruptcy. Many suffer physical problems due to overwhelming work-related stress. Others distract themselves and suppress their pain with constant event planning, competitive activities, and addictions to romantic books and movies, flirtations, and the Big Events I covered earlier.

I'm not saying that every woman who is thin or who keeps an immaculate house has a secret tucked away in her past. But those are just a few of the characteristics of women who are dying on the inside because they cannot forgive themselves for their past mistakes and because they keep sabotaging themselves in the present. Because they have become so used to pretending that all is well, they don't have a clue as to how to start the difficult process of healing those old wounds and stopping the patterns that are driving them into depression and unhappiness. They cannot forgive themselves and move on because they work so hard at denying anything ever happened at all.

On top of everything, they often don't tell their husbands or friends about their deep fears and secrets, so they are locked even further into pretense. With no Christian support group to allow them to be honest about their mistakes and failures, they just go to church and keep on pretending. But at home, they make the lives of their husbands miserable, or they live with a man who makes them feel worse about themselves than they already feel.

Sometimes they leave the church altogether and die a slow spiritual death, starving for meaning to their existence and the joy that they cannot find because they are cut off from God.

Are you already lost like this? Are you beating yourself up all the time because of your mistakes and failures? Are you looking for but never finding the self-forgiveness, love, and attention you need because you doubt your inner beauty and value as a woman? Are you afraid to tell anyone because you cannot bear to admit you have been living in the shadows all of your life, pretending that you were the "good little girl" that your parents always thought you were?

Keep reading, my sweet friend. There is a way out of your house of mirrors.

CHAPTER SEVEN

LOST IN THE DARK WOODS

For I know the thoughts that I think toward you,
says the LORD, thoughts of peace and not of evil,
to give you a future and a hope.

—Jeremiah 29:11

When I sat down at the computer to write this chapter, I stared at the blank page for hours thinking and praying about what I could say so that you would feel loved and comforted by my words. More important, however, I wanted to convince you that there is hope.

I prayed that the Lord would show me how to help you put the past behind you and embrace a new way of thinking. Long after this book is published, I will continue to pray that I have successfully addressed these painful issues. I know how terrible it feels to be lost, especially because of foolish mistakes and bad choices. And I know how difficult it is to find our way back to God and forget the memories that continually remind us just

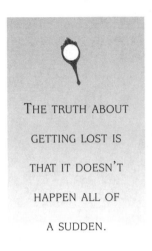

THE TRUTH ABOUT

GETTING LOST IS

THAT IT DOESN'T

HAPPEN ALL OF

A SUDDEN.

how far into the deep woods of despair those bad choices can lead us. Some of you are living with the consequences of your mistakes right now. Some of you are still wandering around in the darkness.

But since you are reading this, I'll assume you're trying to find the light once again. Perhaps you had an affair, but you can't forget it. You may still feel horribly guilty about an abortion. You might have married the man your parents and friends warned you about, and now you're suffering the consequences of your rebellion.

There are far more of you out there than most of the church is willing to admit, primarily because many churches don't know what to do about the problem except to preach and to counsel women to pray harder and read the Bible. If that were all that was required, none of us would ever have gotten lost in the first place, would we?

Perhaps you are still in an affair and can't find the courage or the emotional strength to end it. Maybe you are anorexic or bulimic, and you are still throwing up your dinner when no one is looking. Perhaps you are a young woman who is still struggling with issues from your adolescence and cannot forgive yourself. Maybe you have a daughter you are having difficulty parenting because of your own issues. You could be a young single mother dating without too much discrimination or a divorced woman having one casual sexual relationship after another.

You might even be the "other woman," waiting desperately for that fine Christian man you love so much to leave his wife so God can bless your union and you can be together forever as you think he surely must have intended.

You go to church, but deep inside you know you are not living a life that pleases God.

Whatever the reason you are lost, let me assure you,

I love you.

God loves you.

But you do not love yourself.

WHY WE GET LOST

There are so many reasons we get lost, but let me start by naming the most important.

First, of course, there is just our basic bent for sinning. Chances are you've heard most of your life what a bad person you are. You are eaten up with shame and guilt, but that didn't keep you from sinning. If anything, it just made you so angry and hardened that you didn't care anymore. You just went ahead and did it anyway.

WE DON'T LOVE OURSELVES ENOUGH OR BELIEVE IN OUR WORTH AND BEAUTY ENOUGH TO TRUST GOD'S VOICE.

The truth about getting lost is that it doesn't happen all of a sudden. We take one step at a time—little teeny-weeny baby steps into that Magic Mirror—in such small increments that we don't see the trap that has been set for us inside. We don't see the darkness of the forest on the other side of the mirror. All we see is the shining reflection that draws us in.

Like the queen, pretty soon we are plunging headlong over the cliff to our deaths—if not physically, most definitely emotionally and spiritually. We follow that mirage because we don't love ourselves enough or believe in our worth and beauty enough to trust God's voice instead of that voice coming from the mirror.

Some of you aren't in a terrible situation. Perhaps you don't think you need to read this part. I hope you do read it because

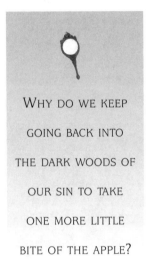

WHY DO WE KEEP GOING BACK INTO THE DARK WOODS OF OUR SIN TO TAKE ONE MORE LITTLE BITE OF THE APPLE?

it's good preventative medicine. Some of you are just depressed, tired, and discouraged. You feel like there is nothing on the horizon to give you the motivation to keep plodding along. You've not made serious mistakes, but you're not experiencing the joy of life either.

But perhaps you are one of the women who is in a terrible predicament. Perhaps you have been blessed with a loving friend who knows how difficult your life has become, but she doesn't know how to help you.

She is trying to convince you that you need to come out of the darkness before it is too late. For the sake of this discussion, I am going to assume that you do realize that you are in a terrible place and you are ready to find your way home.

Whatever your situation, I pray that you have the courage and strength to take hold of what I offer you here and use it to change your life.

WHAT KEEPS US ENTANGLED

I don't think getting out of the darkness is the hardest part. This is especially true if we have managed to come partly out of the darkness without really asking God for help. Even if we have asked God for help, though, breaking free from the lure of the darkness is difficult.

The hardest part, however, is resolving not to go back to check on the things we left behind.

Ask any recovering alcoholic or nicotine addict. It is not the quitting that is difficult. They will tell you they have quit a hundred times, often for years at a time. Not starting again is the really hard part.

Not convinced? Then think about losing weight and eating healthily. I've started hundreds of diets, often losing as much as twenty pounds at a time. Figuring out how to stay thin is the real killer.

Likewise, it is not uncommon for a woman to sit in my office after the love affair ended, crying because she is still fighting a yearning to call and hear the voice of the man she said good-bye to, even when she knows her relationship with her husband, her children, and with God is on the line.

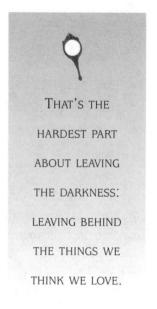

THAT'S THE HARDEST PART ABOUT LEAVING THE DARKNESS: LEAVING BEHIND THE THINGS WE THINK WE LOVE.

Nor is it uncommon for me to see a girl in my office who got pregnant while still in high school and had an abortion. She has been shamed and is thinking she is a terrible person, yet instead of turning to the Lord for help, she becomes even more promiscuous. It is as if a girl believes that because she has taken one bite of the apple, she is poisoned forever. Or she replays the same old sad story, this time hoping for a different outcome.

Why don't we realize that behavior just makes our pain worse? Why do we keep going back into the dark woods of our

SIN BECOMES

AN ADDICTIVE

CRUTCH FOR

GETTING THROUGH

THE PAINFUL

REALITIES OF LIFE.

sin to take one more little bite of the apple, even when we suspect that it is making us sick?

There are a hundred reasons, and right at the top of the list is that old Enemy who sends hordes of his evil helpers to entice, harass, and conspire to woo us back into the darkness. If you don't think there is a constant plot to try to keep you tangled in the thorns and briars, just try getting out, especially without any help.

The minute you start a diet, someone brings a plate of brownies to your door for no apparent reason. The day you vow to quit smoking is the very day that the only seat available in your favorite restaurant is in the smoking section. You're trying to quit drinking, and for the first time in your memory, your neighbors ask you over to their house to barbeque. When you are offered a beer and try to decline, they refuse to take no for an answer. You break up with a man you know is bad for you; then you run into him the next day at the mall. Of course, he asks if you will have coffee with him, just to talk things over. You look in his eyes and melt.

And so before you know it, you are skipping right back into the woods once more, even if it is just to camp out for a little while. Suddenly you remember how much fun you had getting lost. And those scary shadows of shame and guilt don't seem quite so menacing anymore. In fact, at that moment they actually seem quite exciting.

A plot of the Enemy? You got that right, girlfriend.

But I'm not one who believes "the devil made me do it." Quite to the contrary, I am the first to tell my clients that one sure sign of maturity and emotional wellness is to quit blaming God, the devil, their parents, or old boyfriends for their own bad choices and carnal natures.

Most people understand there are powers influencing them that they feel helpless to fight. They know all too well what Paul meant when he wrote, "For we do not wrestle against flesh and blood, but against principalities, against powers, against the rulers of the darkness of this age, against spiritual hosts of wickedness in the heavenly places" (Eph. 6:12).

People know exactly what those "powers" are that are hiding in the shadows, pulling them back in. They deal with them every day, and even if they don't really understand or believe in spiritual warfare, they can feel it.

Each time they have tried to escape the darkness, they have failed not so much because they like being there, but because they are afraid they will leave part of themselves behind. That's the hardest part about leaving the darkness: leaving behind the things we think we love.

YOUR PAST IS

A PART OF

WHO YOU ARE.

The Darkness Is Addictive

In the beginning, at least, the darkness is a whole lot of fun for most people. Just about every wrong thing we do is pleasurable for a short while, and often those wrong things appear innocent and beautiful at first. Most assuredly, they offer comfort, relief from boredom and anxiety, and distraction from problems. Sin becomes an addictive crutch for getting through the painful realities of life. We are so uncomfortable with that word. *Sin.* Just saying it makes us feel guilty. But the truth is that the word doesn't always refer to bad things we do. The word *sin* really describes a state of being. Sin is what happens when we take a step away from the Light and toward the darkness.

SUPPRESSION DEMANDS THAT WE SEEK PLEASURE TO MEDICATE OUR PAIN.

Sin is alienation from God. It doesn't mean that we are bad or defective. *It means we are alone.* And we don't know how alone we really are until it is too late to avoid the terrible consequences of our choices.

The irony is that for a short while sin allows us to feel connected to something bigger than ourselves. It feels exciting, adventurous, and for a young person, very grown-up. When we first go out into the world as adults, we think we know it all and can handle anything in our own power. And because sin is so intensely exciting at first, it is addictive. It makes us feel powerful to rebel against our parents, to make our own choices, and to forge new identities for ourselves.

If we suffered painful adolescent experiences, this exciting behavior becomes the drug we use to stifle our painful memories or to help us forget the things we were taught. Sometimes we believe we can leave our old selves behind altogether. But that is when we truly do introduce pain into our lives, to degrees that we never could have imagined.

You cannot disconnect from your past and go through life pretending painful things never happened. Oh, you might be able to do that for a while, perhaps for many years. But the truth is that your past is a part of who you are. Until you embrace it as your story, restore yourself into right relationship with God, and realize you are no longer the person who did those things all those years ago, your past will haunt you. The longer you try to suppress it and pretend it isn't there, the more it will grow. It will become like a cancer inside—the kind of cancer that you don't know is there until you are already dying.

Suppression demands that we seek pleasure to medicate our pain. The more we seek pleasure, the more inner pain we create, so we must intensify our pleasure-seeking behavior in order to suppress our pain. That creates a terrible treadmill of alternating pleasure and pain, with the pain becoming greater and the pleasure becoming less intense all the time. After a while, we can no longer separate what brings us pleasure and what brings us pain. That is when we become really lost.

Did you know that every time you go back to dabble in the fun part of darkness your brain produces chemicals as powerful as cocaine? That's why sin is addictive.

Even if you just step back into the edge of the woods for a few minutes, your brain responds by zapping your pleasure centers. Just hearing your old lover's voice on the phone, buying something when you are already deep in debt, or eating a quart of ice cream in the middle of the night causes your brain to produce chemicals as powerful as a street drug. Sin squirts a little of that old pain medicine out, and for a little while you don't quite feel so lonely, bored, or angry.

To a lesser degree, those same chemicals squirt when you eat that brownie, smoke that cigarette, drive too fast, or buy that new blouse you didn't need just because it made you feel good to have something new. Those chemicals even squirt a little when you gossip about your neighbor, flirt with a coworker, or when you drive ten miles over the speed limit and think you won't get caught.

It's those little squirts that get you in trouble. The more you do these things, the more you need to do them to keep the hits coming. Pretty soon you're in so deep you feel you could never escape even if you wanted to. You no longer experience pleasure without also experiencing pain. Then you cease to experience any pleasure whatsoever.

That is when some women begin to punish themselves in highly self-destructive ways.

JULIE'S STORY

Julie came to my office seeking counseling for severe depression and bulimia. The thirty-four-year-old woman was beautiful, with long blonde hair and big blue eyes, though she was about thirty pounds overweight. She had been married for about thirteen years to a man she described as "a good man," but one who was passive, boring, unromantic, and emotionally unavailable. Julie claimed he fell asleep in front of the television every night and rarely spent time with her on the weekends. The couple had seven- and nine-year-old daughters, and Julie worked in a large corporation as an executive assistant. The job demanded she work long hours and the commute through city traffic was very stressful.

The couple attended a Protestant church, Julie sang in the choir, and many people often told her that she seemed to have an ideal life.

An only child, Julie described herself as being like her father in nature—passive, quiet, and well behaved. Julie's mother was a housewife and much more outgoing. Julie admitted as a child she and her mother were close, though they were now emotionally distant. She described her mother as rather cold and removed, and somewhat dominating and critical.

After a thorough social history and questions about her early childhood, Julie admitted her problems started when she was molested by a seventeen-year-old male cousin during a weekend visit by the boy's family in her home when she was twelve years old. Because she had admired her cousin, she had let him touch her breasts and genitals. She felt terrible after the incident was over and afraid he would tell what had happened. Since her mother had not discussed sexuality with her daughter, Julie did not understand that even at her age, it was normal to become aroused. It didn't help that she started her period the day after the incident. For years she secretly dreaded her periods because they reminded her of the abuse.

Thinking she was bad, as Julie matured she became somewhat promiscuous, even though by all outward appearances she seemed to be the ideal daughter—active in her youth group, a good student in school, and a cheerleader.

However, Julie was caught up in a deep, internal struggle. She wanted desperately to be the perfect Christian girl, but then she would fall in love with a boy, often an older male, and she would lose her sense of direction. She would sneak out of the house late at night, skip school, and throw caution to the wind to be with the boy with whom she was so infatuated. She often had sex without using protection because she never planned to be bad. In her way of thinking, if she didn't use birth control, she didn't have to admit that she planned on having sex. Only bad girls planned to have sex, but good girls could fall in love and have sex if they were swept away. If they did nothing to stop the event from happening, it was because they "couldn't help it."

Inevitably, Julie's parents would find out about Julie's behavior in the worst possible ways. A teacher would call and her mother would find out she had missed school. On one occasion, a phone call came telling her Julie had been in an automobile accident while skipping school with a boy. On hearing the news, her mother became very emotional and distraught. She did not realize that Julie's behavior and sexual acting out were related to early sexual molestation, and Julie still continued to keep her secrets.

Things improved when Julie left for college. She admitted she stopped dating for several years, attended church faithfully, and was the perfect student. However, over a period of time, she turned to food for comfort.

Obsessed with her weight, she began to diet and take pills to control it, or she would force herself to throw up after meals. Of course, when she lost weight she decided to begin dating again. Once more, she fell into a pattern of risk-taking and sexual promiscuity, even while she was active in her church.

Finally, when she was twenty and in her junior year of college, Julie had an affair with a married professor. Desperately in love, she had a breakdown and had to drop out of college when the professor ended the relationship.

At the time, Julie was too ashamed to turn to her parents for help or to admit she had been living a dual life. She found a job in a large city across the country and began to detach from her parents. She quit praying or going to church and focused totally on building a new identity for herself. She was sick of the internal struggle between the good and the bad Julie. She did everything she could to forget her past, cutting herself off from anything that reminded her of the old Julie. However, she became overweight once again, but this time she developed an anxiety disorder. She often fought thoughts of suicide, or in her words, "just wishing I wouldn't wake up in the morning."

But Julie continued to convince herself that everything was just fine. In spite of her problems, she eventually met Andy, a nice young man in her apartment complex. Julie told him she was "experienced," but she did not divulge the details of her secret struggles. Andy was overweight and seemed to understand Julie's eating disorder. Julie found comfort in his passive, gentle nature. They lived together for about a year, and married two years into their relationship.

The couple bought a house, and Julie had their two children without major incident, except for a few random bouts of unexplained depression and bulimia. There was one particularly deep depression after a miscarriage early in the marriage, but after a while, it subsided. Andy urged her to seek counseling, but she refused.

Julie suffered from particularly strong premenstrual syndrome and often had to go to bed for several days before her period because she was so tired and in so much pain. She would often cry for hours for no reason and throw temper tantrums. She ate voraciously, purged herself by inducing vomiting with her fingers, and bled copiously for days at a time once her period started. During those times she would become very angry. She often stated that she needed more attention and romance but that Andy seemed oblivious to her need. He continued to gain weight, and the couple's marital difficulties escalated.

During a joint marital session, Andy revealed that he had become numb to Julie's mood swings and physical problems. He had learned that if he ignored her and waited things out, she would become her old self. He worried about the bulimia and admitted he was turned off by the thought of his wife's purging. Andy admitted he did not understand Julie at all. The relationship had become strained, but both loved each other deeply and neither wanted a divorce.

A few years into the marriage, both Julie and Andy had begun to attend a large nondenominational church in their community. Julie started working on her relationship with her mother, who was losing a battle with breast cancer.

Julie had never told anyone about her early sexual experience with her cousin or the shame-inducing sexual acting out that had frightened her parents. She had never told anyone, including Andy, about her reasons for dropping out of college.

YOU CAN LEAVE
THE DARK WOODS,
AND YOU DON'T
HAVE TO GO BACK
INTO THAT EVIL
PLACE EVER AGAIN.

At the beginning of therapy, Julie no longer enjoyed sex, hated her body and her weight gain, and was often angry and tired. She had recently been thinking that she was a bad mother and that the only way to solve her problems was to end the marriage and let Andy raise their daughters. Often she fantasized about wanting to die.

Counseling focused on getting to the root problem of Julie's internalized shame and perception of herself as bad throughout her adolescence. Julie realized her early sexual experience had been frightening but that her sexual response had been normal. She was relieved to learn that much of her PMS was aggravated by her emotional reaction to her cycle and an undiagnosed medical problem. When she realized it was unhealthy to see herself as a bad person who pretended to be good, the internal struggle, which had held her captive most of her life, ended.

Julie was able to accept that all human beings contain the capacity for both good and evil and that both of those aspects of ourselves are part of the human condition. She had to learn that the path to emotional health was in accepting and forgiving herself and her mother.

By keeping her distance from God and her parents, Julie had been able to pretend for a while that the past had not happened or that it didn't matter. She was able to avoid confronting the shame she felt about her sexual promiscuity. In the process, in an effort to keep out the pain, she had become numb to any other emotion except anger.

Medication helped with the mood swings, and talk therapy helped Julie realize that she wasn't bad and her parents hadn't intended to shame her—they were simply frightened because her behaviors had been so dramatic and risky. They did not understand what was happening to their only child.

Finally, Julie was able to visit her mother, tell her the things she'd always kept secret, and forgive her mother for not realizing that there had been deeper problems that needed to be addressed. Ironically, before her death, Julie's mother confessed that part of her fear was based on the fact that she had gotten pregnant with Julie out of wedlock and had been too ashamed of herself to discuss these things. Thus she had overreacted to her own daughter's sexual behaviors.

Julie told her husband about her sense of shame and how she secretly believed her earlier miscarriage was God's punishment for her being a bad person. Andy was encouraged to cooperate in a program of healthy eating with Julie and to avoid passivity and withdrawal as a coping mechanism. Julie's bulimia stopped, and she was able to begin a healthy diet and exercise program and resumed a healthy sexual relationship with her husband.

TAKING THE FIRST STEP

Perhaps your particular darkness has not gone this far. Perhaps just one of these things has you feeling as if you are being strangled by the creeping vines, briars, and thorns that have entangled you in a dark woods of your own making. It doesn't take but a few wrong turns to get lost.

To make it worse, the whole time Satan is whispering his sibilant sordidness into your ears. He is constantly telling you that you are trapped and that it is too late to go home. He tells you that you might just as well enjoy it, since that is where you are and that is all you ever deserved anyway.

But Satan is a liar. You don't have to stay in the shadows. You don't deserve it, no matter what you have done. You can leave the dark woods, and you don't have to go back into that evil place ever again.

Please do not be afraid to seek help. Even if you are in the middle of a moral dilemma of some kind, a good therapist will not judge or condemn you. If you happen to go to someone and all he or she tells you is to read your Bible and pray harder, find someone else. Unfortunately, there are counselors out there—many of them Christians—who are not well trained and who confuse preaching with counseling. Don't give up just because you have an unpleasant experience with the first one you visit.

WE ARE TOO ASHAMED TO HEAR ALL THE BEAUTIFUL, COMFORTING THINGS GOD WANTS TO WHISPER IN OUR EARS.

Often a medical doctor will help. A good doctor, particularly a female, should help you find a good therapist as well. Always seek therapy if you need medication for a psychological problem. Never stop medication without discussing it with your doctor, either. And never be too proud to take the medication prescribed for you. Taking medication for a psychological condition is no more a sign of weakness than taking blood pressure medication if you have high blood pressure. Though medicine may help, it should never be used to avoid addressing the real issues that are causing your pain.

Likewise, a good therapist should be able to work with you to find a doctor to help you with the physical problems. You can contact the Christian Care Network at the American

Association of Christian Counselors (www.aacc.net) to find out which Christian counselors in your area are licensed and certified, and which specialize in marital and family problems. It is important that you take care not to seek counseling from those who simply call themselves Christian counselors but who are without the appropriate credentials. There are many people who have

NOTHING YOU'VE DONE IS SO BAD THAT HE WILL EVER QUIT LOVING YOU.

had painful life experiences themselves and they are wise counselors. But those who are not well trained can often do more damage than good.

Also, be careful of which pastors you choose. I've listened to countless women in my office who've had bad experiences with pastors who told them all they had to do was submit themselves to their husbands in order to be happy, even when their husbands were beating them or drinking themselves into oblivion every night.

Certainly do not be lured into a confidential discussion of your emotional problems with your pastor, especially without his wife or another female leader present in the session. This is unethical and often leads to the formation of inappropriate emotional connections that can, and often do, lead to extramarital affairs that can destroy both of your lives. Remember, too, that one big problem in churches can be a lack of confidentiality. Many mental health issues are considered to be medically confidential, meaning it is illegal for counselors to share that information with persons other than yourself, even your husband, without a signed release of information and consent form. Many churches don't understand this and don't educate staff or lay counselors in such matters.

But what if your problem isn't medical or physical? What if it is spiritual? What if you are so far from God you don't even know where to start the process of returning home?

LEAVING THE FOREST FOREVER

The first place we are most often told to go is to the Word, which is absolutely correct. But sadly, oftentimes when we are really lost and confused we make the mistake of picking up our Bibles and reading randomly. Frequently, that approach will lead to the Old Testament, where the picture we're given of God's nature is often that of a wrathful, just, omniscient Being. Or we immediately read the part about the whores, adulterers, fornicators, and thieves.

Not exactly comforting.

So we slam the big Book shut and shudder, too scared and guilty to even try to read it again for another six months or so—sometimes for years. We are too ashamed to hear all the beautiful, comforting things God wants to whisper in our ears. After a while, we become too hardened and numb to feel the warm balm he wants to pour out on all our shame, guilt, and sorrow. We do not understand how badly he wants to bind up our bleeding hearts.

In order to find your way out, there are some important things you must realize. Please get out your Bible, dust it off, and let me reintroduce you to the Person who will lead you back into the Light. These are the Scriptures you need to read. For your ease in reading, I've paraphrased them all from the New King James Version.

For the woman who has put her faith in Christ,

- God is ready to forgive you when you're ready to turn back to him (1 John 1:9).

- He will not condemn you because he came to rescue you (John 3:17).
- He already knows everything you are doing (Hebrews 4:13).
- God is able to help you escape from your situation, no matter what it is (1 Corinthians 10:13).
- Nothing you've done is so bad that he will ever quit loving you (Romans 8:38–39).
- He will never be unkind to you (Isaiah 54:10).
- Faith is the only thing that brings healing (Luke 8:43–48).
- God will be so overjoyed when you come back to him that he will throw a joy party in heaven (Luke 15:7).
- No matter how far you've wandered, when you're ready to turn back, God will bless you (Luke 15:22).
- We can come daily to God for cleansing, and he will remove the dust we've picked up along the way (John 13:10).
- No matter how much damage has been done, God can make something good come out of it (Romans 8:28).
- God has the power to remove our ugliest stains (Isaiah 1:18).
- Satan cannot steal you from God if you have already committed your life to Christ (John 10:29).
- Your accuser, Satan, will one day perish for all his lies (Revelation 12:10).

Remember, God loves you. It's time you started learning to love yourself.

PART THREE

SHATTERING THE MIRROR

CHAPTER EIGHT

YOUR ORIGINAL DESIGN

I have redeemed you; I have called
you by your name; you are mine.

—Isaiah 43:1

𝒥 first began to conceive of my Original Design ideas somewhere around my fiftieth birthday. After coming through more than a decade of great loss, financial difficulty, and just plain hard times, God began to restore my emotional and physical health, endow me with fresh vision for my art and writing, and renew my deep gratitude for the "wonderfully and fearfully made" creation we all are. To me it was nothing short of an epiphany.

At the time, my husband and I were living in the mountains of North Carolina, but we both had recently found jobs in a small town in the foothills about thirty miles away. He'd had to give up his remodeling business due to a hard, snowy winter. After several months of being out of work myself, I had recently started my new job as a family preservation therapist in a county mental health center.

The commute was very difficult, causing me to have to travel some of the most dangerous mountain roads in that part of the country. We both knew we would need to move closer to our jobs. But we hated to leave the mountain village we so dearly loved. I remembered our excitement as we'd packed our moving van and headed to the high country to fulfill a lifelong dream of living in the Appalachians. We had even picked out a house plan for the log cabin we wanted to build. But now, too soon, we were being forced to leave.

It was as if our lives had come to a dead end. After months of being out of work, we were both starting over with new careers in a new town where we knew no one. Even our children had grown up and gone away to live their own lives. We had no family to speak of close to the small town where we were moving. We couldn't understand why God seemed to be taking everything away from us. But it was apparent that at least for the time being, this move was his will.

Even though I was grateful to finally have a good job, I was mentally and emotionally exhausted from years of working in agencies where some of the people working there seemed as confused as the clients they served. I'd helped many people through the years in those agencies, but still, my work was difficult.

One spring day I drove around after work in the new town to check out a couple of rentals listed in the newspaper. Neither seemed too promising. One of the houses was enormous—an elegant three-story Tudor mansion that I knew was way beyond our budget and not even practical for two people and a little dog. The other house was quite small. Though painted in quite garish colors, the house sat in a neighborhood that bloomed with glorious flowers, and had its own secluded garden in back.

So I decided to investigate it a bit more since it was the only affordable house available at the time.

I called the realtor and learned where a key was hidden. A preemptory tour of the little house only confirmed my fears. The rooms were dark and small. Whoever had decided the color scheme on the outside of the house had employed the same heavy-handed techniques on the inside.

But I'd always been somewhat of a gypsy and figured we would only have to rent the house until our old house sold. Then we'd decide what to do next.

It couldn't be that bad. But my heart sank, nonetheless.

Tired, I returned to my car, slid into the front seat, and let my head fall back heavily on the car seat. In spite of my earlier attempts at cheerfulness and bravery, I could feel the dark tendrils of depression begin to coil around in my anxious, fretful mind.

All I could think of was how my bones ached and how much I dreaded the upcoming move. I couldn't imagine myself living in the house I saw before me, either. The longer I sat, the sadder I became. I was so lonely and so tired—too tired to start over yet another time, especially at my age. How I wished we didn't have to leave our little mountain town, but we just couldn't make a living there.

I had had so many dreams that had never come true. So many doors had closed.

My career had stagnated. My writing seemed like a pipe dream. I was an artist with a side business, but I hadn't sold anything in months.

I felt like a total failure.

As I rolled down the car window and breathed in the scents of the twilight garden, I could feel tears slipping down my face. I bowed my head to pray, asking God if this was the house he was providing for us. Deep in my heart I felt that it wasn't, but

OUR VISIONS HELP US TO REALIZE HOW FAR WE'VE STRAYED FROM WHAT WE WERE ORIGINALLY INTENDED TO BE OR DO.

I'd seen nothing else in the paper that day. Nothing but the big Tudor mansion that served only as a faintly mocking reminder of how far my husband and I were from that kind of lifestyle.

I don't know how to describe what happened next except to just tell you and let you decide for yourself whether or not I'm sane.

When I lifted my head, I had a vision. In my mind I saw a little girl standing just a couple of feet away over by large azalea bushes in full bloom. The child appeared to be about six years old, had long blonde ringlets, and wore a sleeveless cotton dress that fell just below her knees.

I knew immediately that the child was me when I was that age.

She looked me straight in the eye, and with a sweet, snaggletoothed smile said, "I'm glad I grew up to be you."

And then she was gone.

Of course, like most of the times God has done something major in my life, I didn't understand then how much impact that little vision would eventually have on me or on others with whom I've shared the story. But in the years since that happened I have traveled an amazing journey. I've accomplished more in the past seven years than in my entire previous career, and I credit a lot of that to the power of that vision.

All this energy came from the vision of myself as a happy child with an enormous capacity for joy, goodness, and love. But most important, that child was proud of me! Hearing her say those precious words healed me of my feelings of failure and anxiety.

That vision caused me to remember what I now call my Original Design.

Since then I've had other people tell me that God has done similar things for them through dreams or healing memories. So many of their dreams contain comparable themes. Our visions help us to realize how far we've strayed from what we were originally intended to be or do. It is as if we had all lost our way in one form or another, and our visions helped us to find our way back home.

My theory is that children are the most natural and unaffected between the ages of six and eleven. That is right before puberty starts with all those troublesome hormones spurting all over the place and right after they become old enough to be aware and curious about the world outside of their own backyards. Unless they've already been abused or emotionally scarred, children at that age are both delightfully innocent and amazingly wise.

WE OFTEN LOSE

GOD'S VISION

FOR OUR LIVES.

We have to go back to our beginnings in order to find our Original Design. This is kind of an inverse of the inner child therapies used by many psychologists these days. Those therapies focus on healing the inner child of adults who were wounded in some way when they were young. My therapeutic approach calls out the often-forgotten happy memories of childhood to minister to the wounded adult and suggests that if we had fairly normal childhoods, those memories can be keys to wholeness.

Somewhere along the way, we lose our happy child. But I don't think she goes away for good—she just goes into hiding. By taking just a few steps in a direction that deviates from what God intends for our lives, we change the course of our lives.

Some of us begin talking to the Magic Mirror. Lost without our happy child inside of us, we invite an unhappy child to take charge. That unhappy child brings her adopted mother with her—the perfect woman we think we must become. That woman is our idealized version of what we should be according to the world's standards, not God's. Her perfection can never be attained, no matter how much we try to become like her. She is the part of us trapped in the Magic Mirror.

In order to free the happy child waiting inside us, we have to say good-bye to our unhappy child and her parent, the perfect woman. Neither one of them was sent by God.

If you have lost your way over the years of living out the expectations everyone else had for your life, or if you accommodated in order to be popular or successful by worldly standards, then you might find great release in remembering your Original Design.

God can change and redirect us any time he wants, even into old age. Also, when I speak of our true nature, I'm not talking about the age-old argument between the proponents of Original Sin and the advocates of the "all children are born good until someone teaches them bad" theorists.

The true nature I'm describing is the part coded into your genes: the personality, interests, talents, skills, and abilities God gave you at birth. I'm not talking about your propensity toward good or evil. That is a different argument altogether. I am talking about the innocent happy child you were before the world robbed you of joy and self-confidence.

I chose the prepubescent age because that is the age when most children know how to play, love God wholeheartedly, and are less concerned with what others think about them. Children have the wonderful capacity to envision their futures with wild abandon, and they imagine themselves doing fearless things. They never worry if what they dream of doing when they grow up is practical, financially lucrative, or socially acceptable. Children never seem to doubt that with God we can do all things.

But as we age, the doubts set in. We begin to question ourselves and God. We become aware of our personal weaknesses and the financial limitations of our families. We lose our joyous, spontaneous worldview and adopt a more cynical, skeptical, peer-oriented worldview. We worry and take too seriously the criticisms and discouragements of others around us.

And that is when we often lose God's vision for our lives. We start doing things not because we truly enjoy them, but because they elicit praise or attention from others.

We quit writing stories because a teacher criticizes us too harshly or because we are told that we will never make enough money as a writer. When someone asks us what we want to do when we are grown, or where we want to go to college, we learn to modify our thoughts and answers so that our responses will reap approval.

We pick a career just because it pays a good salary, not because we have a passion for the work. We go to the beach for a week when we really wish we could work on an archaeological dig in a remote country. We buy a house in a suburb when we'd rather live in the country. We listen when others tell us that we cannot do certain things because we are too poor, too short, too fat, or too uneducated. We settle for a limited life.

And we stray further and further away from our Original Design.

I loved to go fishing when I was a child. My family lived on a farm and we had a wonderful pond stocked with bass, perch, and "spots." There was nothing quite like the surge of excitement in feeling that tug at the end of the line and waiting for just the right moment to snatch it up. The smell of the wet fish flopping on the bank and the feel of the burning sun on my back is just as fresh now as it was fifty years ago.

For most of my life, I didn't ever go fishing. But I try to go fishing when I can now and have often taken foster children on therapeutic fishing trips. Just being outside near a pond is enough for me, and if I can afford it, one day I want to build a cabin overlooking a pond for my writing retreat.

For one of my workshop participants, remembering her childhood caused her to walk barefoot in a creek when she felt

GOD CAN BRING

YOU BACK TO

YOUR ORIGINAL

DESIGN IN GENTLE

WAYS THAT ARE

NOT DESTRUCTIVE

OR HURTFUL.

like she should be doing office paperwork. Normally, the kind of person who would never frolic in a creek when paperwork needed to be done, she found the deliberate stroll in the icy creek bed just the kind of rejuvenating break she needed to restore joy in her work.

For another, it was getting up the courage to start writing stories again.

Yet another realized that as a child, she had wanted to be a missionary, so now she joins mission teams for a week or two at a time once a year. The most surprising change I've seen is one woman who decided to actually get up the courage to travel to Europe and write a book.

That woman was me!

I have created a series of questions to guide you through a visualization of what your Original Design may have been and to help you begin to find constructive ways to move back closer to what God initially intended for your life. The Inventory appears at the end of the book in the resource section.

However, you may feel you are already living authentically. You are not unhappy; you just want to live more abundantly. Even if you find yourself in this category, you'll benefit from the exercises as well because they will help you to stay focused, grounded, and more true to your God-intended life. You may find riches you've forgotten you had.

The Inventory is designed to do more than just get you to do fun things or recall happy childhood memories. It is meant to make you think about how you might not be living in a manner that is authentic to God's original purposes for your life. Hopefully, it will jump-start you toward thinking about how you might have listened more to the world than to your own quiet inner voice guiding you through the years and how that might be contributing now to your distress. It should help you understand better who you really are, what purposes you may have been designed by God to fulfill, and what kind of life you could work toward that might bring you joy and peace. You don't have to run away from home to do this. God can bring you back to your Original Design in gentle ways that are not destructive or hurtful.

This is the voice you should have listened to instead of that Magic Mirror.

I vividly recall telling my third-grade teacher that I wanted to be a teacher and that I wanted a master's degree. I don't believe I knew what a master's degree was at the time, but I was a spunky little girl and I'm sure I thought I knew what I was talking about.

I wanted to be a teacher because the only working women I knew as a child were teachers and they all looked good, smelled nice, and were respected in the community. So I figured that was what women did—they got married, had babies, and became teachers.

That teacher looked at me and said something—I don't even remember quite what it was—that made me feel like she questioned my ability to carry out my plan. I do remember that her tone was somewhat snide and cynical. I suppose she

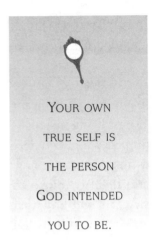

Your own true self is the person God intended you to be.

was jealous because she didn't have a master's degree herself, or because teachers don't like uppity little third-graders. She could have just been tired of hearing me talk. Who knows?

Of course, that only fueled my determination and fed right into my stubborn, prideful spirit. Immediately, my life plan became set in concrete. I was going to become a teacher with a master's degree. No one in my little Presbyterian church ever told me to pray about a choice of careers, and I don't believe I did. Nor did I talk with anyone in high school about my career choice. My parents were encouraging because they felt being a teacher didn't interfere with being a homemaker, and when I was a young woman, being a home-maker was still considered to be the ultimate goal in life.

So I became a teacher. But I hated teaching. I couldn't stand being confined inside all day. I despised the rigid structure and lack of freedom to be creative. I realized that I didn't love teaching—I had loved reading, writing, and the world of books. I loved talking to my students and helping them with their problems. My books and the school environment connected me to people, so I had confused loving school and books with wanting to be a teacher. But I spent more time counseling my students than I did teaching them. So I stopped teaching and became a social worker, then a therapist and now, a professional writer as well. It took me almost half a century, but I did get back to my Original Design.

Of course, it is a rare child who is able to figure out who he or she is at a young age and then remain true to that guiding star. I seriously doubt I could have figured out I was called to be a therapist at the age of eight. I did write a lot, but I never knew any women writers or how to become a writer. Actually, I believe my wilderness wanderings have contributed greatly to my ability to be a good therapist and a better writer.

My husband is one of those rare people who has always known what he wanted to do. He is sixty-one years old and loves farming and building things just as much today as he did when he was a little boy on his father's farm in rural North Carolina. There has never been a single doubt as to what God designed him to do. The unhappiest times in his life were the times he could not do what he loved.

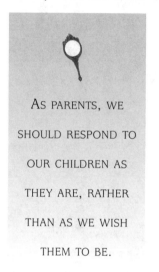

AS PARENTS, WE SHOULD RESPOND TO OUR CHILDREN AS THEY ARE, RATHER THAN AS WE WISH THEM TO BE.

I think women tend to have more problems with this than men. We tend to want to please others more, and because our parents want to protect us, they often guide us based on their own painful life experiences, not God's direction for our lives. They want us to be pretty and popular because they cannot stand to see us in pain. Or they secretly doubt our abilities, so they encourage us to choose safer careers.

Truthfully, sometimes we don't realize what we were called to do until we aren't doing it or until we have chased our own dreams so long that we are worn to a frazzle.

Sometimes it is only in retrospect that we realize what we should have been doing all along. I'm sure when we were young some of us were too immature or unwise to live out our calling. Often we have to stray far from our authentic selves in order to learn.

But that doesn't mean you can't get back on track. It may take time, and it may involve sacrifice, but there are ways to become truer to one's own self. Your own true self is the person God intended you to be, and nothing quite fits in life if you don't find that "flow" that comes from knowing you are in God's will and you have found your right calling. You may think other things will make you happy, but they won't—no matter how much you love the guy, no matter how much money you make, no matter how great your lifestyle.

AUTHENTICITY WILL COME BACK AROUND IN DUE TIME IF YOU LIVE IN OBEDIENCE AND WALK IN FAITH.

A number of women have told me through the years that they don't have a clue who they are or what God intended for them to be. In just about every case, these women had become emotionally frozen at an early age. Because of anxiety or fear, a lack of self-confidence, and no opportunity for self-exploration, they accommodated to whatever others told them they should do. They didn't even know how to begin the process of finding their Original Design. Many couldn't even tell me what they had liked to do when they were children.

In just about every case there was abuse or alcoholism in the family, a critical parent who squelched every dream or talent, or the presence of some kind of anxiety disorder, adolescent clinical depression, or poverty.

As parents, we should respond to our children as they are, rather than as we wish them to be, and we should stop trying to change them. We should encourage them to seek God for direction instead of seeking to impress or please others. We should provide structure, consistency, and discipline so they can explore and learn what it is God has created them to do. We should encourage our children to overcome their obstacles and dream big dreams—in spite of finances, physical limitations, or problems. We should especially choose not to project our own fears and lack of confidence onto our children.

God can change a marriage. He can take those things Satan meant for evil and turn them into good things, and he can use your wanderings in this life to lead you into wisdom and knowledge. Even though I lost my true self for many years, God has used every experience I've had in this life to yield fruit. That is not to say that I'd repeat the bad experiences or the mistakes I've made—no way. The learning at times has been bitter and painful, and God's discipline, though loving, has been harsh. But the experience has definitely not been wasted.

So do not despair. God is certainly in control. You don't have to start all over again to recapture your Original Design. You don't have to change careers, divorce your husband, or blow up your life. Authenticity will come back around in due time if you live in obedience and walk in faith. He will show you how. But it will be in his time, not your own. You just need to cooperate with the process.

Start trying to remember who you were during those precious years. Journal, draw, write stories, and pull out old pictures of yourself. Record any dreams you may have now or dreams you remember from past years. Talk to your family and ask them what they perceived you to be like when you were young. Look at your school record or talk to an old teacher if you have the time. Think about the unique gifts and talents you had then but which you've ignored, suppressed, or taken for granted now.

By the way, we didn't rent the house I looked at that day. A few days later a new ad appeared in the paper for the Tudor house, and, thinking we needed to settle the matter once and for all, I called to inquire about the rental price. To my shock, the house was well within our budget. Not only that, the owners had installed state-of-the-art heating and air, so the utilities were inexpensive. To seal the deal, they wanted renters for only a couple years, because the owners intended to move back in eventually. The situation was perfect for us.

Living in that house helped restore my belief in myself as a person God wanted to bless. It had heavy timber doors, cross-pane windows, and even a butler's pantry. The attached "summer house" included a large ballroom with a beautiful antique glass chandelier. There was room for creating my art once again, and an office I could use exclusively for my writing.

On my fiftieth birthday I put on some music and danced alone in that ballroom, because that was one of the things I loved doing when I was a child. That dance was the best birthday present I've ever had.

I landed my first professional freelance writing project while living there, signed some of my children's stories with an agent, and finally began to make progress toward licensure in marital and family therapy. I'd never had the courage or resources to do any of that before.

I hung a picture of myself as a child right where I could look at her every day ... and remember she was proud of me.

Do you have a beautiful voice but rarely sing? Did you love to pick flowers as a child or walk barefoot in creeks or streams? Were you always playing in the woods, building things, or exploring? Did you love animals, riding horses, playing sports, climbing trees, or pretending that you could fly?

Who were you?

Would that little girl be proud to be you?

HOW TO LOVE A PRINCE WHO NEVER LEARNED TO BE CHARMING (OR THE COMMONER YOU ALREADY HAVE)

*[Love] bears all things, believes all things,
hopes all things, endures all things.
Love never fails.*

—1 Corinthians 13:7–8

By now you've probably figured out that this is not another book about how to save your marriage. Plenty of good books have been written about saving marriages; I've listed many of them in the resource section.

Instead, I want to show you how to love your husband—and by that I mean real love, not just romantic love.

Yes, I'm talking about living with that stubborn and self-centered man who has the emotional sensitivity of a box of rocks; the man who gets on your very last nerve all the time and drives you crazy; the commoner you thought was going to be your prince.

Hopefully, you realize by now that you're no princess, either. I've spent the entire first two parts of this book establishing the fact that this kind of thinking leads to unrealistic expectations of how life should treat us.

And even if you have no plans to leave the man I described above, you might fantasize about it or stay perpetually angry at him because he continually disappoints you. You might wonder why you ever thought you'd be happy spending the rest of your life with him.

One of the biggest complaints I hear from women is they think their husbands expect to be mothered. They are angry because they feel like they have to take care of another child on top of the children they already have.

The irony is that early in our marriages many women do just that and love every minute of it. It is as if we lavish all our years of pent-up nurturing instincts on our new boyfriend or husband. This may last until we realize that he expects it and takes it for granted. When we begin to understand the situation we have created, we stop doting and start complaining, criticizing, and correcting.

Women tend to be verbal processors. Many of us find that we get relief by talking through our frustrations and feelings. But we run the risk of talking about our feelings so much our husbands begin to think we are having PMS round the clock, not just once a month. We talk so much our husbands tend to quit listening, because they think we are just being emotional. When we feel we are not being heard, our frustrations turn to hostility. We get on a downward spiral emotionally, relationally, sexually, and often spiritually. This harms our marriages a great deal.

If we were asked whether we deliberately meant to harm our marriages or hurt our husbands, we'd be horrified at the thought. But that is what we do. Our husbands become more stubborn, more distant, more insensitive, and less invested in the relationship. They shut down and tune us out. And that is the beginning of the end.

THINGS THAT DON'T WORK

Here are just a few things that can sabotage your relationship with your husband. You

- criticize, nag, whine, and pick at him;
- make sarcastic jokes about him in front of others;
- complain about him to your mothers, daughters, sisters, aunts, and girlfriends;
- complain about him to others in front of him or within hearing distance;
- flirt with other men in front of him in an attempt to get an emotional reaction;
- scream at him;
- complain constantly about the lack of money;
- continually infer that you would like a bigger house, a better wardrobe, or things you know he cannot provide;
- neglect to praise him for helping on the few occasions when he does;
- expect him to read your mind;
- go behind him to correct

WE FALL INTO THE TRAP OF BELIEVING THAT IF OUR HUSBANDS LOVE US, THEY WILL WANT TO CHANGE TO PLEASE US.

the things he does (such as housework) because they
don't meet your standards;

- need to be right, have the last word, or qualify
  what he says to others;
- mother him or treat him like a child;
- use negative body language to express your feelings,
  such as rolling your eyes or sighing with exasperation;
- interrupt him and/or do not let him tell his side
  of a story;
- tell him constantly that his version or perception
  of things that happened is incorrect;
- tell him he is stubborn, lazy, or never listens;
- cry and ask to talk about your feelings all the time;
- try to force him to talk about his feelings;
- manipulate him to say "I love you";
- try to force him to prove how much he loves you,
  but you're never satisfied with the things he does
  to show his love;
- direct him to do things instead of asking him to
  do things;
- beg for attention and get angry when you don't
  get it;
- manipulate him with sex, food, and/or money;
- imply that he is intellectually inferior to you;
- apologize for him to others in front of him and
  laugh at his mistakes;
- make excuses and don't honestly confront unac-
  ceptable behavior;
- suppress your anger over big things, then blow up
  over little things;
- fail to discuss things directly, honestly, and neutrally;
- constantly analyze your own feelings and use your
  husband as your therapist.

Boy, that is a boatload of information, isn't it? Who among us hasn't done those things? We do those things because we are frustrated, unhappy, and believe we can change our husbands if we just talk hard enough. What happens is actually the opposite. We lock ourselves into power struggles with our husbands. Instead of changing, they just become more determined to stay the same.

WE NEED TO ACCEPT THE FACT THAT THERE ARE HUGE DIFFERENCES IN HOW MEN AND WOMEN THINK.

We fall into the trap of believing that if our husbands love us, they will want to change to please us. Therefore, we tell them over and over what they are not doing that is making us so unhappy. All this does is reinforce the feeling in men that they are not being respected by their wives and that their wives are trying to control them. I suspect it is a pride issue, but most men can't stand for a woman to tell them what to do. Some get hostile and just as verbally aggressive as their wives, if not more so. Others become more passive, as if they are lying low waiting for the storm to pass. But men like this often become passive-aggressive. They find more subtle ways of maintaining the balance of power, while managing to appear calm and controlled. They may be late to an event they did not want to attend, forget important things, and procrastinate to the point that their wives feel as if they are going crazy.

When our husbands still don't get the message, we employ other destructive strategies, like spending a lot of money or initiating fights—complete with all the drama we think the situation deserves. In their attempts to get their husbands' attention, some women have an affair.

All those methods are destructive. And all they accomplish is to make men feel like small, powerless boys, because those misdirected behaviors are the very things that made him angry at his own mother, or they remind him so much of the negative things he saw in his own parents' marriage. Many men become intimidated by women and angry when they feel we are treating them like children or that we are trying to direct them or control them.

We need to accept the fact that there are huge differences in how men and women think. The irony is that men want women to be more like men emotionally, and women want men to be more like women emotionally

Our differences are initially very exciting, but they are not necessarily a formula for an easy marriage.

Often, the most difficult marriages are those where the husband and wife were initially attracted because they were opposites. So not only are they dealing with gender differences, they are also dealing with major personality differences as well.

Opposites Attract, Then Drive Each Other Crazy

Our differences are initially very exciting, but they are not necessarily a formula for an easy marriage. Marital compatibility studies have shown over and over that men and women who share similar personalities actually have fewer conflicts and express a greater degree of marital satisfaction than those in marriages where couples report themselves to be opposites, or at least very different, in many areas of interest. However, often opposites report a higher "sizzle factor" in the relationship initially.

Quite honestly, my husband and I have to work hard at this problem. We are polar opposites. I am fiery and verbal, while he is passive and quiet. When I'm troubled, I want to talk through the issue with another person. Sometimes this is the only way for me to understand why I'm feeling what I'm feeling.

Although I am not a perfectionist, I am definitely an over-achiever and often feel driven to reach my goals. I struggle with wanting to accomplish tasks quickly so I can mark them off my list and get on to the next project. I struggle with ADHD (Attention Deficit Hyperactivity Disorder), and I can become disorganized and overwhelmed by my varied interests and multiple pursuits if I am not careful. On the other hand, when my husband is troubled, he withdraws and works things out on his own. If I try to force him to talk about things before he is ready, he becomes sullen and irritated. He gets upset when I flood him with a torrent of words, primarily when I throw out angry, half-formed thoughts and impulsive accusations. Feeling inadequate to help, he shuts off emotionally and withdraws.

Because he is so introverted, he has difficulty remembering to communicate with me. Truthfully, I believe he could easily live like a hermit in a cabin in the woods. In addition, he's a bit messy, passive, and complacent about the "honey do" jobs around the house, even though as a talented carpenter he can build or repair just about anything with his hands. Fiercely independent, he has never liked to be told what to do. Thank heavens he has been self-employed most of his life and has never really had to take orders from other people!

After years of struggle, we now both realize that when we do not make a definite effort to communicate effectively, we will misunderstand each other's motives and intentions because of how differently we think and process information.

We make the mistake of presuming to know what the other is thinking and then make false assumptions based on inaccurate information. When we go too long without purposeful and healthy communication, we become distant and disconnected from each other emotionally.

WHY OPPOSITES ATTRACT

Opposites tend to attract for many reasons. Initially, being with someone so different from yourself can lend great mystery and a sense of novelty to the romantic process. This can create an intense physical chemistry. Also, if we feel we're lacking in some area, we often marry a person who we feel offsets our perceived weaknesses. I was very attracted to my husband when we first started dating because he seemed so reserved and mature. His quiet strength and unruffled calm seemed the perfect balance to my impulsiveness and sometimes-excessive emotional reactions to life events.

On the other hand, I think he was attracted to me because he felt shy and awkward and liked being with someone who could draw him out and provide adventure and excitement.

But when opposites marry for these reasons, we sometimes set about to change the person to be more like ourselves instead of accepting our spouses as they are, because we find it so difficult to connect on so many levels. The very traits that initially attracted us to each other as sexual partners are still there, but we badly miss those things that would make it easier for us to be good friends.

DIFFERENT PEOPLE, DIFFERENT PERSONALITIES

According to the Kiersey Temperament Sorter, a test used by many psychologists and therapists to determine personality and temperament styles, the world is divided into sixteen basic personality types. It is the combination of characteristics from those types that describe the entire population of humans, both male and female, to some degree. Just do a search for personality tests (Kiersey Temperament Sorter, Myers-Briggs Personality Inventory, etc.) and take one to see which of the personality combinations best describes you. The Kiersey test is free and available online. It is comprised of seventy questions that render amazingly accurate, scientifically calculated results. They are designed for use by the individual, and do not require analysis by a trained counselor.

It can be valuable to know, for example, that an extrovert is energized by verbal processing with other people, but that an introvert is often drained and overwhelmed by it. This is a common problem I encounter in marriages when the wife is exasperated because her husband won't talk with her about things she feels are important, primarily her emotions and their relationship.

Emotional, sensitive, creative people think a lot about ideas and view the world differently from people who primarily see the world in terms of logical thought, facts,

THE BEST TWO THINGS TO DO ARE TO GROW SPIRITUALLY AND TO BECOME EMOTIONALLY INTELLIGENT.

science, and numbers. The former tend to view relationships as being the reason human beings were made. Also, they place more importance on how something looks and feels.

The logical, factual person tends to view humans as created to fulfill a function in the world—beings designed to get a particular job done. Relationship is nice, but not the most important thing. Feelings? They don't think about them much at all unless forced to by others. People like this are also more interested in how something performs rather than how it looks or the feelings that it evokes.

Think about this in reference to your marriage. Suppose you are a person who views relationships and feelings as the most important thing in the world, but you are married to a man who believes that the job—how we function—is the most important thing. You will be the woman who wants to sit and talk with your husband all the time about feelings, and he will think he is doing a great job at being your husband just because he shows up on time, puts bread on the table, and keeps the grass cut.

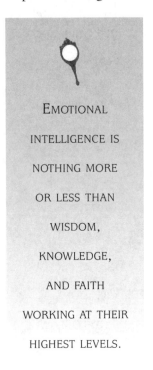

EMOTIONAL INTELLIGENCE IS NOTHING MORE OR LESS THAN WISDOM, KNOWLEDGE, AND FAITH WORKING AT THEIR HIGHEST LEVELS.

You don't feel as though you have a relationship because you aren't talking. But he thinks he is doing just fine because, after all, isn't he still with you? Isn't he giving you his paycheck? Isn't he having sex with you on a regular basis? What more could a girl possibly want?

Most typically, this is the guy women stereotype as being all about sex, food, television, and sitting on the john. And truthfully, that is not a totally inaccurate picture.

But it doesn't mean these men are not intelligent, thinking, complex creatures. It just means they think with their heads instead of their hearts, and feelings just aren't all that important to them. Getting their physical needs met is primary, because that's what they believe allows them to function on a daily basis in a stressful world. They want to function well, because that's how they show their love. That is what makes them happy, so they assume it makes you happy as well.

They don't have a clue about what to do when you start crying and talking about your feelings. They feel like helpless, inadequate, miserable failures. Then they get angry and shut down because they cannot fix things for you.

If you are trapped by illusion and romantic thinking, your problem may be worsened. You will find it difficult to live with a guy who is not sensitive or romantic, or who doesn't know how to meet your excessive emotional needs. Sometimes you'll feel like you are starving to death emotionally.

So what do you do? The best two things to do are to grow spiritually—which I will discuss in the last chapter—and to become emotionally intelligent.

EMOTIONAL INTELLIGENCE

Daniel Goleman wrote a wonderful book titled *Emotional Intelligence* (New York, Bantam, 1995). His research indicates that those who understand, assess, and appropriately control their emotions early in life are those most likely to achieve success in work and relationships. He further states that emotional intelligence is a greater indicator of success in life than the raw intelligence quotient (IQ).

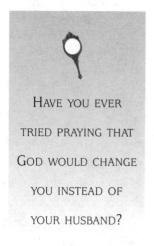

HAVE YOU EVER TRIED PRAYING THAT GOD WOULD CHANGE YOU INSTEAD OF YOUR HUSBAND?

This was an amazing piece of research given that the secular arena has often placed more emphasis on academic achievement than on wisdom and maturity—attributes the Bible urges us to pursue.

Notice I didn't say successful people become unemotional. Emotions are good things. But there is such a thing as being too emotional, and we can allow our emotions to dominate us to the point that we cannot make logical decisions or relate well to others. As a result, our lives can become roller coasters.

Clinical mood disorders are sometimes at the root of excessive emotionalism. If your emotions swing wildly from one extreme to the other—from depression to giddiness—or if you suffer depression, especially for more than two weeks at a time, then you need to see a doctor.

Symptoms of depression are sleeplessness or sleeping too much, changes in appetite (eating too much or not eating at all), excessive fatigue, loss of interest in things you used to enjoy, and periods of crying or deep sadness. You can learn about other symptoms at www.mentalhealth.org.

WOMEN CANNOT CHANGE MEN; ONLY GOD CAN CHANGE MEN.

The Bible is full of admonitions, particularly in Proverbs, about the folly of allowing feelings—despair, irritability, lust, anger, fear, sadness, jealousy, insecurity, and all the emotions that flood us—to drive our life choices and interactions with others. Emotional intelligence is nothing more or less than wisdom, knowledge, and faith working at their highest levels. Medicine can stabilize you so that you can be wiser and less fearful and anxious, but it won't change your inner self. You have to work on that yourself. Medication can, however, help stabilize you enough to begin that process in an intelligent manner.

There are wonderful new medicines to help your condition that have fewer side effects than some that used to be prescribed, and research is revealing new information all the time about biochemical changes in our bodies.

You are not crazy. But if you've been programmed throughout your life to think romantically, and you've formed false belief systems in childhood, it is more likely that you will not be as emotionally intelligent as others. You will feel constant insecurity, emotional pain, and a yearning for the "something more" I talked about earlier.

Actually, bright, creative types often have the most difficulty overcoming their emotionalism and moving beyond their past shameful mistakes and failures or the abuses and attacks they've sustained. More sensitive than others, their pain runs deep and their emotions tend to be more volatile and difficult to handle.

How do you become more emotionally intelligent? Therapy can help. Reading the Bible is essential because it grounds you in truth and washes your brain of false belief systems. Finding friends (the subject of a later chapter) who challenge you to think logically rather than emotionally is a key factor. But there is nothing quite like good old-fashioned practice too. It takes awhile, but if you make becoming less emotional a goal, you can achieve it. Go to a doctor and rule out a mood disorder. By all means, ask God to show you how to become less emotionally reactive.

If my guess is correct, most of you are praying that God will change your husband so he will meet your emotional needs. Have you ever tried praying that God would change you instead of your husband?

ONLY ONE WAY TO CHANGE HIM

There's only one way to change a man, and that is not to try.

Women cannot change men; only God can change men. The irony is that often men *do* change once their wives accept them just as they are. The basis of true love is acceptance.

I am not talking about ignoring him or pretending he doesn't have flaws. I'm talking about embracing the man he is instead of the man you want him to be. Not only that, I'm saying you need to build him up, praise him, and concentrate on the good things about him. Meanwhile, you need to work on changing the things in yourself that need changing.

This does not mean you roll over and allow him to abuse you emotionally or physically, or that you let him off the hook if he is truly selfish, rude, thoughtless, and unkind. But instead of trying to manipulate him emotionally, you need to communicate in a manner that is as firm, clear, neutral, and straightforward as possible. Set your limits and establish clear boundaries about what is acceptable behavior.

If that doesn't work, then take action.

Taking Action

Far too many unhappy women talk and complain about how their husbands treat them, but they actually do very little that is positive to teach their husbands to behave any differently. Unfortunately, women who do this often parent their children the same way—they threaten, cajole, complain, and throw temper tantrums. With children, we use time-outs. You can sit children in a "naughty chair" like Super Nanny does, but you can't exactly sit husbands in the corner, can you? Yet most women try by denying sex, giving their husbands the cold shoulder, or laying a guilt trip on them with tears and pleading.

For example, I hear a lot of women complaining because their husbands won't pick up after themselves or help with housework, even though these women have full-time jobs just like their husbands. Even if they don't work outside the home, wives resent it when their husbands drop a wet towel on the bathroom floor when the hamper is just an arm's length away, or when they leave dirty clothes all over the house. They feel that it is disrespectful and thoughtless. Personally, I agree.

But the mistake they make is thinking their husbands will quit doing these things if they just complain enough. This is not true. The only way to get husbands to start doing these things is to *quit doing them yourself.*

But a lot of women tell me this doesn't work. I then tell them to take *loving action.* You tell your husband that you have decided to quit picking up after him and that if he cannot put the clothes in the hamper he will need to wash his own clothes from now on. In fact, I often counsel couples to each do their own laundry. Being a stay-at-home mom doesn't necessarily mean you have to become a maid. You have plenty to do for those in your family who cannot look after themselves. In fact, I tell parents to teach their children to do their own laundry as well, just as soon as they are old enough to learn.

But if you decide you like doing his laundry, wash only those things that make it into the hamper. He'll get the idea when he runs out of clothes. Dirty dishes? Then choose not to cook food that uses a lot of dishes, or use paper plates.

This is not to punish your husband. It is not about manipulation, having the last word, or refusing to exercise your "servant spirit." By all means, if you feel God is telling you to bless your husband by doing his laundry, then listen to God. But if you are angry and feel that you are being treated like a maid, that is not healthy.

Don't be snide or sarcastic either. It is important to be respectful, considerate, and neutral. Above all, be consistent. Whatever you start doing, keep doing until it works. Don't give up too soon. *And make sure you tell him ahead of time what is going to happen.* It is important that he understand you are not being mean or withholding help, but simply allowing him to make his own choices. Tell him you are doing this out of respect for yourself and your own needs, and that you've decided to take better care of yourself. Tell him you are tired of being angry and that you want to change yourself from now on instead of trying to change him.

But it is critical for you to be fair about the good things he is doing. One of the biggest complaints I hear from men is that when they try to help around the house and do things to make their wives feel loved, it is never enough. Their wives go behind them correcting, fixing, changing, and improving. The men never feel as if they have been praised for the things they do. Nothing will kill a man's desire to help faster than going behind him and redoing what he's done.

THE BEST THING TO DO IS TO TELL YOUR HUSBAND DIRECTLY WHAT IT IS YOU WANT WITHOUT WHINING OR COMPLAINING.

But you may have to face the fact that some men deeply believe it is a woman's job to do these things because their mothers did. There are quite a few men who will wear dirty clothes and don't mind a messy house at all.

I suspect that a lot of women don't mind the actual work of picking up after their husbands as much as they mind men's attitudes that somehow, if men help out, they are doing women a special favor, but if women are doing it, then that is their job. That is the deep issue that upsets women— the fact that their husbands take for granted that housework is their wives' job—even though the women also work outside their homes.

If that is the case in your household, you may have to be really firm for a long time. Or you may have to compromise and settle for negotiating a peaceful agreement that works for the both of you. Just remember that all your actions should be loving.

You are not trying to change your husband. You are trying to change your own response to your husband's behavior.

Women Who Want a Mind Reader

One of the myths I frequently hear from women is that if a man loves her he will know what she wants and needs. In other words, true love should result in a sort of mystical union where communication is almost irrelevant.

How often have I heard these words: "If he really loved me, he would take the time to learn what I need (want, like, desire, enjoy, etc.), and he would give those things to me without my needing to ask"?

This type of woman wants her husband to be the nurturing, sensitive, and emotional kind of man who anticipates what she likes and gives it to her. She wants her husband to think like a woman! But what she doesn't realize is that most men just don't have that kind of intuition or nurturing ability. They didn't learn it growing up, and most don't come by it naturally. And if her need is constant and consuming, then he is going to easily tire of trying to figure out what it is she's seeking. If nothing he does is ever good enough, discouragement sets in. Soon he will just give up altogether.

The best thing to do is to tell your husband directly what it is you want without whining or complaining. One good example is how my husband and I handle Christmas. Long ago we gave up trying to surprise each other. Instead, on Christmas Eve or the day before, we go out for a special dinner and shopping. I choose my gift and he chooses his. We are always happy with what we give each other!

Tell your husband what you want for your birthday, remind him of it the day before, and tell him when you'd like to get flowers or be taken to dinner. Especially tell him when you are feeling in the mood for sex.

I just finished reading an entertaining, well-written novel by a famous writer. She writes primarily for women in midlife.

It was enjoyable to read, but I realized that, like the stories of many contemporary writers of women's novels, this book was about finding the perfect soul mate—a man who is perfectly intuitive, thoughtful, and financially well-off enough to buy wine, flowers, and extraordinarily thoughtful gifts at a whim. And, of course, he is always good-looking. They live in a fairy-tale cottage of some sort, and there are rarely any stupid mistakes, financial failures, or body odors with which to contend.

FOR MOST MEN,

ROMANCE AND

SEXUAL INTIMACY

ARE INSEPARABLE.

Give me a break.

MYSTICISM AND ROMANCE

You can fool yourself all you want about the mystical experience of romance, but from a man's perspective, the ultimate goal of romance is to prime a woman for sex. Men think of romance as something they have to provide in order to get you in the mood. They do not love you any more or less because they are not being romantic—they are just being realistic about the end result.

But many women want romance without the sexual obligation, because they secretly believe in the romantic ideal, think sex is a bit crude, or have low sex drives. I've often heard women say, "I just want to cuddle, and he ruins it by starting to grope me. It makes me feel so devalued—like all my husband wants is sex. He never wants to just spend time with me."

Of course, most women who say this are young, and their husbands are galloping, lusty young steeds with hair-trigger "love buttons." But women of all ages have idealized the romantic experience so much and are in such strong denial about what romantic stimulation does to men that they do not see the biochemical truth that, for most men, romance and sexual intimacy are inseparable.

I cannot truly speak for men, but from what I've learned I believe many men ascribe a mystical quality to the sexual experience itself if they love the woman and are expressing that love in a sexual manner. Physical union with a woman makes a man feel loved, special, affirmed, appreciated, and connected to his wife on a more profound level. Romance can help make the trip to the bedroom more fun and exciting, but it is not what meets a man's emotional need. In fact, the more a man loves a woman, the more he needs to show that love by having sex with her. That's just the way men are neurologically designed.

WOMEN AND SEX

Stereotypes from the Victorian age support the myth that all men crave sex and can't get enough—and that most women, except those who are depraved nymphomaniacs, really don't enjoy sex at all. These stereotypes still haunt our perception of what constitutes a normal sexual relationship in a marriage, especially in Christian homes where sex might not be discussed very often in any real way. I suspect very few adolescent girls, Christian or otherwise, ever get enough information about what constitutes a normal sex drive for women. This leads to shame and self-doubt in young girls who are experiencing strong sexual impulses at relatively young ages—something that is actually quite normal.

Many women enjoy sex as much if not more than their husbands. In fact, evidence suggests the number of women with high sex drives is increasing.

This may be a result of chemicals in our food and hormones in meat products, or on the other hand it may be due to improved nutrition and health care. It certainly could be related to constant exposure to sexual programming, romance novels, and suggestive movies. Personally, I think it is the combined effect of all those things.

One thing we do know is that certain proteins and hormones are produced by fatty tissues in the female body that increase sex drive. Weight gain increases the production of those hormones. Weight gain also figures highly in poor self-image.

The combination of low self-image and increased sex drive can cause conflicting emotions, frustrations, and could be one explanation why many women report an increased dissatisfaction with themselves, their sex lives, and their lives in general.

On the other hand, depression can kill sex drive. So can a lot of the medications used to treat depression, which not only decrease sex drive, but also increase weight gain. That can produce a lot of stress in a marriage.

Whatever the reasons, I am dealing with an increasing number of marriages where both men and women complain about their sex lives.

Regardless of your sex drive, compatibility with your husband is the issue.

A medical specialist or certified sex therapist can do wonders toward restoring harmony and balance in your sex life. Please don't be embarrassed. It is a problem many have from time to time. Your sex drive, or lack thereof, is primarily a biochemical function. It is not a character flaw. Let a doctor or a therapist help you.

There are ways to get our emotional needs met other than through our marriages. Christians frequently turn to the church to fulfill these needs. But what if your relationship to your church is unhealthy too?

CHAPTER TEN

CHRISTIAN FAIRY GODMOTHERS

"You will soon see the Prince at the ball, and he will be enchanted by your loveliness! But remember that you must come home at midnight, for that is when the spell ends. Your coach will turn back into a pumpkin, the horses will become mice again, and the coachman will turn back into a horse. You will be dressed again in rags and wearing clogs instead of these dainty little slippers! Do you understand?" Cinderella smiled and said, "Yes, I understand!"

—Paraphrased from the traditional folktale "Cinderella"

*T*he children of Israel had a habit of turning to the wrong people for solutions to their problems.

In the days when the Israelites were held captive in Babylon, there was a group of women who claimed to have occult powers. Not only were they charming and fun to be around, but they were cultured and well dressed. They exuded grace and style. They knew everybody who was anybody and could drop names of all those who were in positions of power at the time. They made a fine art of ingratiating themselves into wealthy households by promising peace and prosperity to all who supported them. They knew how to use their powers of persuasion and manipulation quite well.

The only way we'll inherit the kingdom is to bring everything we say and do under obedience to Christ.

These women offered magic charms, spells, veils, incantations, and special "secret" prayers to captivate their admirers. They claimed to have visions from God that always promised good things. It didn't matter how corrupt or sinful their audience was—God was going to deliver them all!

Two well-known prophets of the day, Ezekiel and Jeremiah, attempted without success to convince the Israelites to turn away from these false prophetesses. These men prophesied the destruction of Jerusalem because the Israelites would not turn from their lust, greed, idolatry, and worship of pagan gods. And history proved them correct.

Ironically, the Israelites thought the prophecies of Ezekiel and Jeremiah to be terribly exciting and entertaining, and would actually show up anytime the two addressed a crowd. They would nod in agreement and appear to take the prophets' words to heart, but in truth, the only words they paid attention to were those of the false prophets and prophetesses because those were the "easy words." But Ezekiel warned the Israelites that God hated these false prophets and called them "soul-hunters" who preyed on his people.

> Woe to the women who sew magic charms on their
> sleeves and make veils for the heads of people of every

height to hunt souls! Will you hunt the souls of My
people and keep yourselves alive? (Ezek. 13:18)

Just as Ezekiel predicted, when disaster did finally come,
the Israelites had no faith upon which to lean because they had
no real relationship with God. Many succumbed to panic,
depression, and physical and mental illness.

The magic did not hold up to the darkness of the midnight
hour.

The same is true today. When God doesn't answer our
prayers in our timing or reassure us with "easy words," we have
a tendency to turn to false prophets who tell us what we want
to hear. But the truth is that no prayers or special prophets can
give us shortcuts to the kingdom. The only way we'll inherit
the kingdom is to bring everything we say and do under obedience to Christ. This is true even for those of us who've been
handicapped by a lifetime of magical thinking.

Many times we try to play "fairy godmother" to other
Christians as well. Just like the false
prophetesses in the book of Ezekiel,
some counselors or church leaders
have been known to give false comfort
to those in difficult circumstances.
Instead of encouraging women to
build a strong relationship with God or
helping them understand the hard
truths of Christianity, some hand them
a sugarcoated gospel. Women are told
that if they just pray harder, submit to
their husbands, and do the work of the
church, everything will be fine.

But I have not found that to be
true—not for myself or for most of

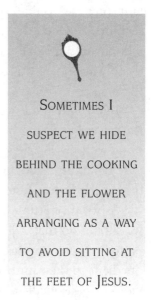

SOMETIMES I

SUSPECT WE HIDE

BEHIND THE COOKING

AND THE FLOWER

ARRANGING AS A WAY

TO AVOID SITTING AT

THE FEET OF JESUS.

the women I know. That message is different from what Jesus told Martha when she claimed Mary wasn't doing enough to help her when Jesus came to visit.

> As Jesus and his disciples were on their way, he came to a village where a woman named Martha opened her home to him. She had a sister called Mary, who sat at the Lord's feet listening to what he said. But Martha was distracted by all the preparations that had to be made. She came to him and asked, "Lord, don't you care that my sister has left me to do the work by myself? Tell her to help me!"
>
> "Martha, Martha," the Lord answered, "you are worried and upset about many things, but only one thing is needed. Mary has chosen what is better, and it will not be taken away from her." (Luke 10:38–42 NIV)

The nurturing role women play in the church is an important one. I would not be a Christian without the strong servants of God who taught me the gospel through Sunday school, music, Bible studies, and church fellowship. I believe those who spread the gospel are doing exactly what God wants them to do.

But I also think women sometimes avoid the real call on their lives by staying busy with projects that may not have anything to do with spreading the gospel. Sometimes I suspect we hide behind the cooking and the flower arranging to avoid sitting at the feet of Jesus.

As for submitting to husbands, it is true that the Bible says we should do that. I just think that the word is often misinterpreted. Often Scripture is used to imply that women should be obedient to their husbands regardless of how ungodly, unrighteous, or disobedient to God those men are. We can hide behind our husbands to avoid Jesus just as easily as we hide behind staying busy with church.

However, one of the translations of the word *submission* in the Greek is *hupeiko*. This use of the word is actually a military term, which has more to do with job function than the exercise of power for the sake of power (*Vine's Expository Dictionary of Biblical Words,* Nelson, 1985). The use of the term implies that marriage

FOCUS ON PLEASING GOD, NOT YOUR HUSBAND, AND LET GOD TAKE OVER CHANGING HIM.

has a mission, and the woman's job is to help in the fulfillment of that mission. Of course, those in the military must obey their commanding officer. But in the family, God is the commanding officer, and the husband should be in submission to God.

God called Adam to take care of the garden, and he created Eve so that Adam would not be lonely and so that he would have someone helping in the mission of caring for the garden. In order to do that, Eve's relationship with God needed to be just as strong as her husband's.

Perhaps that is why Eve got into trouble. Male or female, our call is to submit to Christ. A strong relationship with God must be formed so that we understand our mission. If both husband and wife are fully submitted to Christ, there will be unity.

WHEN HUSBANDS WON'T PRAY

From what I hear, not many men actually pray with their wives. They may be praying to God and reporting back, but they are not praying *with* their wives, at least not as often as they should.

I suspect some men worry that their wives are secretly analyzing or critiquing their prayers. Some men have admitted that they don't pray because their wives give them the impression that they believe themselves to be spiritually stronger than their husbands. Others admit they've turned spiritual growth into a kind of power struggle with their wives.

All of these things may be factors, but often it is a matter of personality and communication styles as well. Introverts often don't like to pray aloud, and men who feel themselves inarticulate are often afraid to admit their fear of praying with their wives.

YOUNG WOMEN CAN "FALL IN LOVE WITH JESUS" AND EXPERIENCE THE SAME EMOTIONAL RUSH THAT THEY DO WHEN THEY FALL IN LOVE WITH A MAN.

But what if you know your husband is not living the life God wants and this makes you sad and anxious? What if this makes you question your husband's ability to lead you spiritually? The truth is that you can't make your husband grow in the Lord. You can only concentrate on growing in the Lord yourself. But you don't have to enable your husband's behavior or submit to those things that you know would be sinful in God's eyes. Focus on pleasing God, not your husband, and let God take over changing him. And find a church that helps you to do just that.

Unfortunately, too many women settle for churches that don't challenge them, or they look for pastors who will parent them like fathers or give them the attention they crave. This can be spiritually deadly for the woman trapped in romantic thinking, especially if those pastors are lonely and vulnerable themselves. It is easy for a woman to fall deeply in love with a man who offers to pray with her—especially when her husband won't—or who seems to have great empathy for her emotional needs. Many lives have been ruined and careers destroyed because of relationships that began in this manner.

In addition, young women can "fall in love with Jesus" and experience the same emotional rush that they do when they fall in love with a man. Just like in marriage, when the honeymoon wears off, the true marriage with Christ must be created. The same thing applies to our relationship with a church. We begin to find fault with our churches, and all we can see is what's wrong with it. We reason that it's easier to leave and start over somewhere else. Or we abandon church altogether.

When a romantic thinker experiences hurt in the church, or when bad things happen in her life, she sometimes reasons that God is being mean to her or has forgotten her. For the same reasons she is unhappy in her marriage, she now feels unhappy in her relationship with God and her church.

CODEPENDENT CHRISTIANS

The term *codependence* is used to describe a relationship in which a person confuses loving someone with needing that person, to the point that she sabotages the personal growth of herself and the other person in order stay in the relationship. It is an unhealthy model for a relationship, because it usually requires dependence rather than personal growth.

The weaker person in the relationship never has to grow up. The person depended upon feeds on the power of being needed in an unhealthy manner. Unfortunately, the stronger person also tends to enable dependent behavior instead of encouraging independence.

In codependent families, children are rescued from the hard tasks of adulthood and are financially supported by their parents long past the time when they should have grown up and learned to live on their own. Mothers especially have a difficult time letting their children grow up because they fear not being needed anymore.

In codependent marriages, the wife becomes dependent on her husband and expects him to parent her like a father. She expects him to fulfill all of her needs, and in return she avoids taking responsibility for herself or learning important life skills.

In codependent churches, just like in dysfunctional families or marriages, the pastor is like a father to his children and dependence on the church is actually encouraged. Church members are fed the "milk of the Word," and they are not encouraged to examine it too deeply or to disagree with the church's stance on any interpretation of that Word. In these kinds of churches, entertainment and social activity devoid of any real spiritual purpose often become the focus.

IT IS SAD WHEN YOU LEARN THAT YOUR ONLY VALUE TO SOME PEOPLE IS IN WHAT YOU CAN DO FOR THEM.

During times of crisis, codependent individuals, marriages, families, and churches tend to fall apart because the weaker members cannot pull their own weight. The powerful individuals become overwhelmed by the demands placed on them to care for the needs of weaker members, and the whole system falls into chaos.

When a larger community crisis strikes, such as a severe economic downturn, churches like this are often empty and silent. Because of the weaknesses in their body, they have few resources to offer the greater community. And because the body as a whole is not spiritually grounded, there tends to be a great deal of inner power struggle, argument over petty issues, and high staff turnover. Tithing is minimal, and whole families leave the church because they sense something unhealthy is going on, but they are not quite sure what it is.

If you are in a church like this, the potential is there for you to be wounded. Even if you're not hurt in any significant way, the likelihood remains that you will not grow significantly. When challenges arise later in life, you won't have the spiritual resources you need to cope.

By and large, most churches are not codependent. The church as a whole is alive and well in America, and it is challenging and empowering both men and women to grow in the Lord. These churches focus on missions rather than entertainment, and they don't get caught up in the power struggles that characterize codependent churches. The

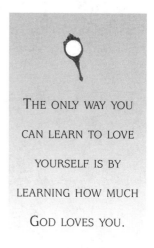

THE ONLY WAY YOU CAN LEARN TO LOVE YOURSELF IS BY LEARNING HOW MUCH GOD LOVES YOU.

codependent church is often a church that is dying because it is caught up in a pattern of crisis management. Because it doesn't encourage the creation of strong young servants to take over leadership of the church, the cycle continues and worsens as time goes by.

I want you to think about your relationship to the church you're in now. I'd like to help you avoid getting involved with a church that falls into this category and find a good church more like I've described above.

Have you transferred the responsibility for your relationship with God from yourself to the church? Do you try to get the church to meet all your emotional needs? Do you enable weaker members by constantly rescuing them instead of empowering them to grow themselves? Have you become burned out because you take better care of other Christians than of yourself? Have you surrounded yourself with those who do not feed your spirit because you are lonely and desperately need companionship, no matter how high the price?

I struggled with codependency for many years because I confused love with dependence. The end result was that I took on way too much responsibility for everything and everybody. I needed desperately to prove my worth by being needed, thus I allowed many family members and friends to become too dependent on me. Then I became angry in later life when they did not reciprocate by allowing me to lean on them when I needed them.

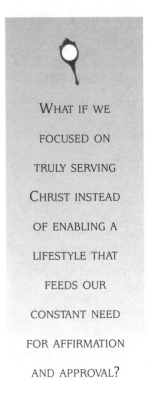

WHAT IF WE FOCUSED ON TRULY SERVING CHRIST INSTEAD OF ENABLING A LIFESTYLE THAT FEEDS OUR CONSTANT NEED FOR AFFIRMATION AND APPROVAL?

I took better care of everybody, including my church, than I did of myself, because deep down I expected I'd receive profound gratitude and appreciation in exchange for all the love and devotion I lavished on others. But that was not the case. Some accused me of being too controlling, while others just took me for granted.

When I realized this, I began to change. I started taking better care of myself. I began to refuse to place myself in situations where others' needs were met at my own emotional expense. But trust me, I encountered great resistance in the process. There is a very high price to be paid for years of codependent behavior. It is sad when you learn that your only value to some people is in what you can do *for* them, not what you do *with* them.

Many Christian women grow up being taught to do this, however, particularly here in the South. We pour ourselves into our roles as wives, mothers, daughters, and friends in an effort to feel loved and needed. Then we become bitterly disappointed when this love is not reciprocated like we thought it would be. We feel used and abandoned. Those feelings turn to anger, and that is often when our bodies become ill.

The truth is that if you don't love yourself enough to take care of your own health, emotional life, and relationship with God, then no one else will either. The only way you can learn to love yourself like that is by learning how much God loves you, and you do that by forming a strong relationship with him.

In return, your relationship with others will be healthier, and you will not need them so much in order to feel good about yourself. You will surround yourself with those who feed your spirit and challenge you in your walk with God. You would rather be alone than surround yourself with those who use you or don't appreciate what you do for them. You will begin to learn that the only thing you truly need is God.

But if you try to get those needs met through your friends, family life, and church, instead of God, you will never be satisfied. I know that I wasn't. In fact, what I experienced was that my stress levels went through the roof and my physical health went to the basement.

STRESS AND THE CHRISTIAN FAMILY

When we see acts of service as a means to earn love, we get into trouble. We find ourselves doing too much and building resentment when those activities don't bring us the results we want. Throw in a tendency toward perfectionism and an addiction to the approval of others, and what you have is a recipe for disaster.

Eventually, you will explode. You will not be able to contain the anger and pain you feel when your spiritual and emotional needs don't get met through all you are doing for others.

You will run to the Magic Mirror. You will begin to reject the harder truths of the faith and opt for New Age philosophies that promise you peace and prosperity. Instead of finding your true calling in the Lord, you will settle for a shallow faith that allows you to justify your addictions.

But your pain will only increase as time goes by.

Granted, it's hard to feel in touch with your spirituality when you are angry about the demands placed on your life, especially when you don't feel supported by your husband emotionally or spiritually. It's even harder when your relationship with God is superficial.

What if we focused on truly serving Christ instead of enabling a lifestyle that feeds our constant need for affirmation and approval? I think we would be so much happier and healthier. I suspect most of our stress-causing activities are centered on gaining the approval of others instead of the approval of God.

One of my pastors used to say that most Christians are "driven" rather than "called." He maintained that when we are called, God provides the energy, strength, and provision we need for the task. There is a divine flow to our work that reminds us the Holy Spirit is in charge. Of course, there will always be spiritual warfare when we serve God, but that's another matter altogether. The stress and problems I'm talking about are those that come when we do things in the name of God that God never called us to do in the first place.

If we are driven by emotional need, we tend to be over-involved in outcomes and desperate to prove our worth by outperforming others both in church and in other areas of our lives. We find ourselves embroiled in disputes, power struggles, and "turf" issues. We are perceived as people who must always be in control of others. Often, we find ourselves competing so that we can feel good about ourselves.

But our God is not codependent. Jesus didn't do things that way, and neither should we.

I'm delighted to say that not all churches encourage codependency. There are many wonderful, healthy churches out there. Don't settle for a church just because it is convenient, because you grew up in it, or because you've got friends who go there. Find a church that meets your needs in the midnight hour.

In that midnight hour it's possible you'll need a good counselor as well.

CHRISTIAN COUNSELING

I am thrilled with the growing credibility of credentialing and training programs for Christian counselors. These days, many good church-affiliated or private Christian counseling programs offer this valuable service to the community.

But not all church counselors have been trained. Many are self-appointed. Unfortunately, some may confuse *rescuing* with *empowering*. They give good advice, but they don't help you learn how to solve your own problems, which is what a good counselor should do. Let me assure you, I am not one of those people who thinks that only certified, licensed counselors can be effective counselors. Some of the wisest counselors I've ever known were laypeople. Programs such as the Stephen Ministries are excellent sources of good counseling.

But sometimes poorly trained Christian lay counselors confuse brotherly and sisterly love with the work of counseling. They fail to set appropriate boundaries and often lack the emotional distance they need to effectively help others. They form inappropriate relationships with the people they are trying to help, and though they rarely intend to cause harm, many say and do hurtful things because they are operating out of their own emotional neediness, not the Holy Spirit's guidance.

Many untrained counselors are codependent themselves and have deep wounds they are seeking to heal through their sacrificial service to others.

YOU MUST FIND

A CHURCH THAT

PROVIDES THE

SUPPORT AND

RESOURCES

YOU NEED.

Unfortunately, because people are often embarrassed to let others know they need a counselor, they don't ask questions about the reputation of a specific person in a counseling role. Do not be afraid to ask a counselor about his or her training. If possible, get references. Start slowly and allow trust to build before you hand your life over to an untrained counselor without question.

But what about the false prophets the Bible talks about? Are there really false prophets at work today?

CHRISTIAN FORTUNE-TELLING

Yes there are, and unfortunately, just like the women in Babylon, they prey on those prone to magical thinking and romanticism. The best thing for you to do is to pray for wisdom and discernment. Avoid people who bring you "a word from God" if that word seems more like fortune-telling. God can certainly inspire others to encourage or uplift you, provide healing, or clarify an issue you're struggling with. But much harm has been done to Christians, women especially, who've been prayed over and had their future predicted.

I've dealt with many sad and discouraged women through the years who ran from one prayer partner to another, looking for a word from the Lord. They were delighted when told that they would conceive a child, find the man of their dreams, get that wonderful new job, or be reconciled to a prodigal in a certain time period. But as the long days passed and the dreams never came true, their joy was replaced by sadness; their hope by discouragement. Many Christians have fallen away from the faith, I believe, because the prophecies spoken over them by well-meaning Christians with a word from the Lord never came true.

Jesus warned there would be so many prophets in the last days of this world, even the strongest Christians would be deceived by them.

True prophets of the Lord—people gifted and full of the Holy Spirit—do exist. Personally, I have had powerful words spoken over me that encouraged me and transformed my thinking. Eventually, some of them did come true. I've been given similar insights to share with others from time to time. But I have given this a lot of thought, and I realize that no special insight ever told me that specific events would come true. The prophetic words spoken were encouraging and comforting, but they did not commit God to a particular wish fulfillment or time schedule. They gave me hope that things would change and that I would survive whatever difficult time I was going through then, but they didn't make specific promises on God's behalf that certain concrete events would happen. The people who spoke those words over me didn't indulge in fortune-telling, and they didn't manipulate me or gain power and advantage over me because of the words they spoke to me.

You may not believe in the exercise of the gifts of the Spirit. You may be a Christian who worships in a setting where traditional liturgy is followed and little emphasis is placed on these things. But you can still be misled by false prophets. They come in many guises.

FALSE PROPHETS WEAR MANY MASKS

Many New Age philosophies have crept into the church, and those philosophies do not encourage a strong personal relationship with God, require personal change, or confront sin. These churches sponsor programs that confuse spirituality and psychology. They subtly enable sin by pretending it doesn't exist. It is almost as if they believe God was created to benefit humans instead of humans being created for God's pleasure.

These false prophets teach that everyone is going to heaven no matter what state they are in; God provides whatever we want (notice I didn't say need); and if we act like good little children, God will give us the desires of our hearts. Those philosophies don't talk much about the evil, despair, and persecution we are going to experience if we truly live for Christ, even though the Bible speaks a lot about those things. Few practice dying to self. Instead, courses are taught on how to get your emotional needs met and how to ensure success and happiness. When the bad times come, false profits don't offer comfort, just platitudes.

If you really want to grow in your walk with the Lord, you must find a church that provides the support and resources you need. You can "church shop" until you find a church that never challenges you to grow and only provides fellowship, entertainment, and comforting words, or feeds your tendencies toward romantic thinking. But you won't find the strength you need for living the Christian life.

THE CHURCH AFTER GOD'S OWN HEART

Jesus reminded us repeatedly that if we want happiness, we have to quit chasing it. Instead, we need to focus on others, but not in a codependent way that expects something in return. We're not to take care of those who are perfectly capable of taking care of themselves, like passive husbands and lazy children, because we want them to love and need us.

You do, however, have to quit thinking about your own narcissistic need for attention and start thinking about others less fortunate than yourself. Once you form a strong relationship with God and love him, you will want to serve, not because it meets your own emotional needs for fellowship and being part of a group, but simply out of love and gratitude. You won't find yourself trapped on a treadmill of service to those who are ungrateful and selfish. Nor will you be angry because you aren't thanked or shown gratitude on a daily basis.

Read Isaiah chapter 58. God tells us very clearly in this chapter exactly what he expects us to be doing.

> Is it not to share your bread with the hungry, and that you bring to your house the poor who are cast out; when you see the naked, that you cover him, and not hide yourself from your own flesh? Then your light shall break forth like the morning, your healing shall spring forth speedily, and your righteousness shall go before you; the glory of the Lord shall be your rear guard. Then you shall call, and the LORD will answer; you shall cry, and He will say, "Here I am." (Isa. 58:7–9)

I thank God for the thousands of missionaries working diligently in the world today to spread the gospel. Hundreds of wonderful Christian programs are reaching the needy in many cities across America. I've worked for a few of them, the Methodist Home for Children in Raleigh, North Carolina, for example.

Likewise, there are hardworking, underpaid pastors in churches all over the nation who exercise their beliefs as the unsung heroes of the faith. They have turned their backs on just about all the world has to offer in order to serve God and his children.

I've been personally guilty in the past of using church as a form of entertainment and fellowship more than as a way to get closer to God and stronger in my knowledge of spiritual things. It makes me sad to think of all the years I wasted playing Christian. As a result, I'm grateful to be involved in a number of projects in my community that are addressing the real needs of those in crisis. One of those is Carolina ChristCare, Inc., a nonprofit I helped found in my community to equip churches to start disaster programs in their own communities. Activities like this bring me great satisfaction. I spend little time doing things I do not feel God has called me to do, regardless of the pressures others attempt to place on me.

If you turn your heart toward God and let him meet your emotional needs, the only approval you will desire is God's approval. Like Isaiah says in chapter 58, your light will shine and your healing will spring forth readily (paraphrased).

To begin that journey toward healing from codependence you will need friends—real friends who know the Lord and can help you grow in your walk with him. In order to have those kinds of friends, you are going to have to climb down from your self-imposed towers of isolation and mistrust and build bridges that form healthy bonds with strong women who know God and encourage you to live the life he has planned for you.

You may have discovered that women like this are not all that easy to find.

But the next chapter gives you a few ideas of where to look and how to act when you find one.

CHAPTER ELEVEN

BUILDING BRIDGES, CLIMBING DOWN FROM TOWERS

Do not let your adornment be merely outward ... rather let it be the hidden person of the heart, with the incorruptible beauty of a gentle and quiet spirit, which is very precious in the sight of God.

—1 Peter 3:3–4

*R*eady to climb down from that fortress you've built around yourself? Ready to shatter that mirror and step back into the real world? If so, you need some girlfriends!

I don't know how I would have survived the past forty years without my girlfriends. No matter what was going on in my life, my best friends have always understood me, and they've been there for me no matter how difficult it must have been at times.

The only downside to these precious friends is that most of them live a few hours' drive from my home. Many lonely Sunday afternoons I wish I could pick up the phone and tell them to get themselves over to my house so we could go for a walk or sit down for a nice long chat over a cup of coffee.

But in spite of the distance, we speak on the phone, drive to each other's homes when we can, and e-mail on a regular basis. We save up our cell phone minutes so we can lament or giggle, depending on the need. They pray with me any time I ask, and I pray for them as well. They know everything about me and still love me anyway. They couldn't care less about those "outward appearances" spoken of in 1 Peter.

Of course, we've disappointed each other from time to time. I'm sure I've hurt their feelings on a number of occasions, because I am blunt and outspoken. Sometimes they frustrate me as well, such as when I see them making mistakes I know will bring them pain or when they nurse attitudes I know will block God's blessing in their lives. But since I do the same thing, I cannot point the finger. Regardless of our mistakes and bad attitudes, however, we all love each other unconditionally. They are my biggest fans, and I am theirs.

We celebrate each other's successes and downplay each other's failures.

We encourage each other when the future seems dim. When one of our children is in trouble, we run to offer comfort and advice. We soothe sadness, wipe away tears, and laugh and act silly when exhausted from daily living.

We love it when one of us loses weight and looks good. And if one gets a new job, goes on a nice vacation, or has a wonderful blessing of any kind, we are thankful and happy. In fact, we help each other find good clothes at bargain prices and give each other little gifts with great meaning to commemorate those special blessings.

We treat each other's elderly parents and doddering relatives with patience. We relate to each other's husbands like the brothers they really are. We don't talk badly about each other to other people, and we don't hold grudges if one of us hurts the other. We either forget the slight, or we confront it with love and honesty. We forget everything and forgive much.

We do not expect perfection in each other's houses, appearances, or actions.

We've seen each other messy and without makeup on more than one occasion. If one is in a bad mood and needs to be left alone to work things out, we know to keep our distance, but we also have an uncanny sense when the other is in emotional pain, and we often call each other just when a friend is needed. We can hoot with laughter over silly things and not worry about looking stupid in front of each other.

To be honest, in my lifetime I've had fewer than five people who fit in this category, and one of those girls died several years ago. I miss her terribly. One is single, another is divorced, and another is married with several children and grandchildren who require daily attention. One has been wheelchair bound for almost forty years. Another is my cousin I told you about in the first chapter.

I have many acquaintances, but very few of them have become my real friends. Some drifted away because of time, distance, or just plain inattention. Some I thought would be my friends for life turned out not to be my friends at all, much less friends for a lifetime.

I have two younger sisters I love very much, and we have a good relationship, but it is not like the relationship I share with my girlfriends. I think that is because of the age differences and the fact that we all three have busy careers and very different personalities.

On the other hand, my girlfriends and I are about the same age and a lot alike. We often say we feel like sisters, but without the sibling rivalry. We share a love of God, art, books, travel, music, and each other's children. Like life coaches, we help each other make major decisions concerning business, relationships, parenting, or just plain life.

Some think us a bit flamboyant, a bit loosely put together. We don't care. We just remind them that God tells us we are supposed to be "peculiar people." I'd say pretty much all of us are on the peculiar side.

Instead of being bound by blood, we are bound by love.

I DON'T NEED FRIENDS WHO AREN'T WILLING TO PUT GOD FIRST IN THEIR LIVES.

I'm a strong woman, and intense. I've had to be to live through some of the things Satan has pitched at me. Because of this, sometimes I'm irritable and cranky and too quick to give advice or point out fallacies in thinking. Sometimes I get very deep. Some women can't deal with this—they act offended, as though friendship should always be light, airy, and fun.

I'm not that kind of person. It is just my nature to be a bit sad at times, perhaps when I'm struggling with some new idea or project being birthed in me by God. The birthing process is difficult for me.

My real friends understand this. But though they are gentle and kind, they let me know when they think I've stepped out of God's will, when I have hurt them in some way, or when I am thinking wrongly about some situation I'm in. They never encourage me to sin, and they always lovingly and gently rebuke me when my words are too harsh or my attitudes are ungodly.

Likewise, they do not praise everything I create. If something I've written is poorly done, they tell me. If something I paint or sculpt is amateurish or tacky, they say it needs work.

I can count on their honesty, but also on the fact they will not be snide, jealous, sarcastic, or meanly critical either. They will not make catty remarks or say things to make me feel stupid or demeaned in any way.

Good friends are hard to find these days, especially if you're like me—a person who wounds easily because I love deeply. I don't accept loss well, and I agonize over the things I could have done better to have saved a relationship. I can get angry and mull over ill-treatment, but in the end I know God expects me to ask forgiveness if I've done anything wrong and to make amends when I can. When there's nothing else to do, I need to let go. In fact, I'd say that one of my weaknesses through the years has been that I hang on way too long to those who have never cared for me as much as I cared for them.

But the older I get, the more I realize I don't need to do that. I cannot control people. I don't need friends I can't count on or who don't care enough about the relationship to work at it. I don't need friends who aren't willing to put God first in their lives or who compromise themselves in ways that make me uncomfortable.

I want real friends. Friends with whom I can be honest, share, and be myself when I am with them. Friends who understand that real friends are hard to find and cherish those they have. Friends who can forgive each other. Friends who will be with me until the end of my days, or theirs.

THE FIRST STEP—

AND THE

HARDEST—IS TO

BE VULNERABLE.

For many of the women who have come into my office through the years, the real root of their problem is loneliness. None of them had real, honest friends. Invariably, when we talked they confided either that they didn't like other women very much or that they were too sensitive and never mastered the art of making friends. I always have to stifle the urge to reach out and befriend these women and show them how it should be done.

Therapy is about inducing change, but friendship is about not expecting the other person to change. Like the best marriages, it is about loving the person just like they are. And really, that is what sustains the best marriages as well. Sometimes friendship between spouses sustains a marriage as much as good sex, children, and shared faith and values.

FRIENDSHIP IS ABOUT NOT EXPECTING THE OTHER PERSON TO CHANGE.

But so many women seem clueless about how to go about having good friends.

The first step—and the hardest—is to be vulnerable.

Women can be cruel to each other. Many of us have been subtly trained all of our lives not to trust other women, but to compete or compare ourselves with them. Letting down our guard and allowing another woman into our hearts and minds is a frightening prospect. There's a chance we'll be hurt in the process many times before we strike gold in the deep mine of relationship. It takes a secure person to reach out and make good friends, and most of us are not that secure.

My best girlfriends showed up when we were all at our lowest points. We were all rather insecure about ourselves because of the traumas we had just suffered. One was in the midst of a bitter divorce from her alcoholic husband. One had just made a difficult transition from the West coast to the East coast because her art business had gone sour. Another had been traumatized by involvement in a cult religion. My low point was that my young brother had just committed suicide.

We were wary at first and slow to warm up to each other. In fact, it wasn't until we all moved to separate parts of the state that we realized how much we had come to mean to each other. I thank God for all of them, because they have each ministered to me in ways I could never have imagined.

WOMEN AND THE COMMUNITY

Not only do women carry distrust for each other, we're also products of a disconnected society. We don't have strong relationships with extended family anymore. We used to have aunts to raise us, or cousins or siblings we could reach for in a crisis. Now we move off to big cities where we don't know anyone and where we expect our marriages to be enough.

Friendships provide additional nurturing and connectedness, a benefit that can take some of the pressure off the expectations you have for your husband. Although your best friend ideally should be your husband, for many women that is not a reality. It doesn't mean you have a bad marriage. It just means that you are going to need to find healthy, mature Christian women to be your friends.

FRIENDSHIP SHOULD BE RESERVED FOR THOSE WITH GOOD MORALS AND STRONG VALUES.

FINDING FRIENDS

Here are a few tips on how to find and make friends:

- Form a strong friendship with God first.

- Pray and ask God to lead you to the friends he would have for you.
- Realize that friends will come and go. Some are for a season, some for a number of years, others for a lifetime. Let go graciously of those who don't seem to value the friendship as much as you do, but stay available.
- Look for shared passions like music, art, children, and faith.
- Be able to laugh at yourself.
- Give friendship time to grow. Water and nurture it. Don't take it for granted, but don't hover over it either.
- Don't be too needy. If you need therapy, find a therapist. Don't drain a friend by always expecting her to listen to your problems without helping with hers.
- Don't borrow money. You can accept a gift, but don't ask.
- People want to be with others who make them laugh and feel good. If you are depressed, get help. Dragging others down will not make you feel better. But a good friend will tell you if that is happening, not just drift off without explanation.
- Don't compete with other women. Refuse to play competitive mind games. Don't try to dress better, impress other women with your achievements, or expect their constant adoration of your talent.
- Don't pursue friendships with women who don't share your values. The Bible tells us to help younger women and teach them, but friendship should be reserved for those with good morals and

strong values; otherwise you will invite chaos into your life.

- Don't rescue other women and then encourage their dependence on you.
- Don't spend money to impress them or engage in activities you cannot afford just to be with them.
- Don't call new friends every day, get jealous if they don't invite you places, or expect them to be your friend exclusively.
- Beware of those who come on too fast. They may be narcissistic, fickle women who will discard you once the honeymoon of the new friendship is over. These are the women most likely to back away when their thinking or spirituality is challenged.
- Don't tell your new friends all your most intimate secrets right away. Let a friendship build over a period of years before you share private information.
- Never talk about your friends negatively to others or spread gossip about them. Never go to another person to discuss problems you should be discussing directly with your friend.
- If a friend hurts your feelings, approach her with honesty and love, without accusation or blame. Take responsibility for your own hurt feelings.
- If your friend is annoying you over and over, let her know it in a loving way, but make sure it is worth the price of hurting her feelings.
- The Bible says to "never take offense." So don't.
- Cherish the friends you have.
- Be thoughtful with small gestures, cards, and remembrances.
- Be there for them when they are in pain, not just when it feels good.

FINDING MENTORS

One of the most important things I've done in my life is to find and cultivate relationships with women who are smarter, more accomplished, and more successful than I in my fields of interest. I've learned through the years that successful women are relaxed, easy to approach, and usually eager to help other women find their way.

Those who aren't approachable usually aren't very nice anyway, and they will only allow you to approach if they think they stand to profit in some way. That is not the nature of mentoring.

You can tell from a distance if a woman is someone you admire and want to be like. You can usually tell from her demeanor whether she is proud and self-centered or warm and approachable.

One time I didn't take my own advice and approached a big New York agent at a seminar where she was speaking. During her presentation, I'd sensed she was a rather cold person with a sharp tongue and withering glance. She seemed elegant and knowledgeable, but also proud and arrogant. Her response to my approach was exactly what I should have expected. But I learned a lot from the exchange, even though it didn't feel good at the time.

Mentoring is not about currying favor with those in power so you can ingratiate yourself and get a piece of their action. That is reprehensible to me and I can spot someone schmoozing a mile away. I don't go after people who are rich and famous because I hope to latch on to their coattails—but I do tell women I like and admire that I need their help with some specific goal. And in every case I can think of, I've gotten it.

Let me give you an example. Many people through the years told me I could write, but mostly they were friends, family members, or coworkers. I finally got up the nerve a few years ago to compile a little book of poems, short stories, and essays, which I eventually self-published.

I worked hard on my book and didn't put it out there until a couple of good critics had looked at it. I hired people to edit it for me. I struggled to find just the right printer, paper, artwork, and layout. Altogether, it took about two years.

When it was finally finished, I started selling it at my seminars and workshops and out of the trunk of my car. I never deliberately marketed it; I just sold it at cost whenever someone asked for it.

One night I attended a reading by a well-known author at a local bookstore. At the time, this author had published fourteen novels. I'd read her books for years and loved her work, but I never dreamed one day I'd get the chance to meet her, much less talk to her or show her my writing.

IF YOU HAVE A SKILL OR TALENT, FIND MENTORS TO TEACH YOU, BEFRIEND YOU, AND SHOW YOU WHERE TO GO NEXT.

After she finished signing autographs and the crowd dwindled, I went up and politely asked if I could get some advice. I wanted to know about the wisdom of pursuing an MFA (master of fine arts) in creative writing. In the process, I told her about my little book. To my surprise, she whipped out her business card and told me to call her at home! I called her in a few days and at her request mailed her the little book. It wasn't too long before she called me back and told me we needed to have a meeting. I couldn't believe it when she invited me to her home, took me out to lunch, and told me I needed to become a professional writer.

That day changed my life. This woman was not only gracious and kind, but she took the extra time to show how much she cared and to encourage me in a special way. She didn't have to do that, because I know for a fact that she is frequently approached by people. I've learned since that she is gracious and charming to all of them, even if she may not say the same thing to each. (If you've never read Lee Smith's novels, treat yourself to one soon!)

I've had other experiences with mentors since then. This book wouldn't have been published without Marlene Bagnull, the founder of Write His Answer Ministries, whom I approached at a writing seminar just like I did Lee Smith. The same is true of Pamela Duncan, author of two successful novels for women. Now I am working on a new book with Melissa Slagle, a therapist and trainer I approached at a training she was teaching at a local university.

ONE OF THE BIGGEST MISTAKES MADE BY WOMEN WHO ARE TRAPPED IN THE MAGIC MIRROR IS SURROUNDING THEMSELVES WITH FLATTERING ADMIRERS.

Women who are successful, like Melissa, Lee, Pam, and Marlene, are secure and able to recognize honesty and courage when they see it. Most will respond favorably if you approach them humbly and with an attitude of respect.

If you have a skill or talent, find mentors to teach you, befriend you, and show you where to go next. Surround yourself with those you admire, and do the things they tell you to do.

One of the biggest mistakes made by women who are trapped in the Magic Mirror is surrounding themselves with flattering admirers who they can impress all the time but who can teach them nothing. You aren't growing if you surround yourself with people who only tell you what you want to hear.

Never Stop Growing

When I talk to women about their marriages and their dissatisfaction with their lives, one of the themes that always emerges is fear: fear of abandonment, fear of not being good enough, and fear of missing out on the things they could have had or done in life if they had married someone else or taken a different path.

The next theme that emerges is boredom. They are bored with their husbands, bored with their activities, and bored with their jobs and the daily grind of life. They are sick of picking up after husbands, settling fights between squabbling children, and having it taken for granted that they will be the one who scrubs the toilet and plans the meals.

When I put these two things together—fear and boredom—what surfaces is the truth that women who feel this way have stopped growing and learning. They have stifled their own creative urges, intelligence, and ambitions in order to create the life they thought they wanted. Most don't know what they want. I believe

ACHIEVING BALANCE

IS DIFFICULT BUT

NECESSARY.

they're looking for excitement, adventure, and growth—but most are going about it in self-destructive ways. Part of the problem is that women who stay at home are often lonely and have too much time to think. Those with small children and little patience don't have the time or energy for much else. Many are perfectionists and wear themselves out trying to keep their homes spotless, while others are so overwhelmed by it all that they become disorganized to the point they can barely function. They have lost themselves in the process of becoming wives and mothers. This is a dangerous time for women who already have secret fears and feelings of inadequacy about how they compare with other women, because they are living in isolation and getting very little positive feedback.

And even if women have interesting careers, they can still fault their husbands for not being supportive enough, not emotionally available to them, or not sensitive to the stress they suffer. For the most part, women like this may grow intellectually, but not spiritually or emotionally. They often don't take care of themselves in any kind of nourishing, self-loving way. They never have fun or take the time to explore life.

Achieving balance is difficult but necessary. When life is out of balance and there is no growth and strength in the major areas of life—mind, body, and spirit—people suffer.

In America we are so ambitious and so focused on appearing successful, we fail to enjoy the process. We don't take healthy risks, we don't learn new things that will challenge us to think differently, and we don't attend to all parts of our being.

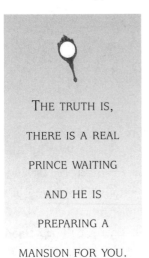

THE TRUTH IS, THERE IS A REAL PRINCE WAITING AND HE IS PREPARING A MANSION FOR YOU.

Every living thing in this world grows. God first created a garden and made Adam and Eve gardeners. God loves growing things. All you have to do is look around you to see that he loves creativity.

God could have built a house in a suburb in Eden, paved the streets, put in a swimming pool and a tennis court, and created a big car for Adam to tool around in.

He could have given Eve her own laptop, but he knew his daughter didn't need it. Instead he gave his children gorgeous sunsets; every beautiful animal, fruit, and foliage imaginable; lots of room to be creative; and lots of places to explore. The only things they needed to do were to stay away from what God told them to avoid, to grow things, and to enjoy their lives.

Just like you and me, they didn't think it was enough.

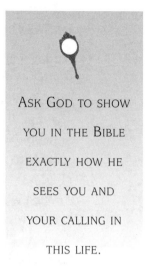

ASK GOD TO SHOW YOU IN THE BIBLE EXACTLY HOW HE SEES YOU AND YOUR CALLING IN THIS LIFE.

I believe everyone has a creative spark and a desire to be brave and adventurous. But women squelch that spark because of fear; and they hide behind the excuse that the demands of home, job, and children have robbed them of money, time, and energy. I recognize those excuses because I used them hundreds of times myself.

If women would stay out of malls and fast-food restaurants, many could have enough money to nourish their spirits in whatever way they need. And if they would find other adventuresome women, they could travel and see the things in the world they want to see. God can provide babysitters and money for art supplies, travel, or college educations.

Our children don't need to be the center of our universe in order for us to be good parents. In fact, I think one of the biggest problems in American households today is parental overindulgence. Moms and dads have allowed their children every advantage and opportunity for growth, while granting themselves little or nothing for intellectual growth and learning. Children can be well educated without taking expensive trips to Europe or having new cars—things their parents never did or had.

I want to encourage you to stop making excuses for yourself and stop expecting your husband to make you feel alive. The truth is, there is a real prince waiting, and he is preparing a mansion for you.

How to Encourage Learning and Growth

- Sit down and make a list of all the things you'd like to do before you die, both reasonable and unreasonable. Pray over them and then pick one to accomplish within the next year. Pick one a year until you've done the entire list. Shift the unreasonable to the reasonable side as opportunity arises.
- Hold a family conference to explain you've stopped growing as a person and you need their help to resume the process.
- Ask your children how they would like to see you grow and improve yourself. Trust me, they will tell you!
- If they say they'd like to see you quit worrying so much, then ask them to give you a specific plan of what they are going to do to help you quit worrying. Write down what they say and ask them to sign it. Discuss what will happen if they don't help you reach your goals or do their part, because without consequences their signatures will mean little.
- If you think you can't write a book, sit down and structure the outline for one. Then write a chapter. Write another chapter every time you think you can't write a book. The fear of writing is the enemy of many called to write.
- Try one basic art class in the medium that interests you most.
- Buy a digital camera and take pictures of everything beautiful you encounter.
- Put a dollar a day in a jar for spending on things that nurture your soul, like good music, books, or

flowers. Treat yourself to that thirty dollars once a month.

- On your lunch hour, go to libraries, museums, and art galleries instead of malls.
- Write an essay about what you really feel God has called you to do. Then write out an explanation of why you haven't been doing it—and why that's going to change.
- Pray that God will give you vision and remove all fear.
- Ask God to show you in the Bible exactly how he sees you and your calling in this life. He will lead you to the appropriate verses in due time, if not immediately.
- Don't be afraid to explore. People don't always know whether or not they are going to enjoy something or be enriched by it until they try it. It is not a waste of money to try new things and then discover they are not what you thought they'd be. Some will accuse you of dabbling, but dabbling is exactly how young children learn. We learn that way too.
- Explore your mind and thoughts by writing them down. Journal once a week, or every day if you can.
- Write a letter to yourself about the kind of woman you would like to be.
- Write a letter to the happy child you once were and ask her what she thinks you need to do differently with your life now. Imagine what she would say.
- If you were not a happy child, write a letter of comfort and redemption to yourself.

- List the ways you sabotage yourself.
- Volunteer to work hands-on with people who make you feel uncomfortable, like the homeless or the mentally ill or severely mentally handicapped. You'll be surprised how much you learn.
- Avoid tourist traps on vacations and go to places that provide learning experiences. Disney World may be fun, but there is little to be learned there.
- Educate yourself, even if you don't take but one course at a time.
- Set a goal of eating nothing but healthy foods for an entire week. You'll be surprised at how good you feel.
- Gradually cut down on caffeine.
- Make a solo road trip to start overcoming your fear of being alone. Make sure your husband understands your goals and supports you.
- Start a Girlfriend's Club. Put a poster up in the library, grocery store, or in a public place as a Christian woman seeking road companions for adventures of the spirit. This can be for travel, cultural experiences, crafts, classes, or just having coffee and sharing dreams at the local coffeehouse on a regular basis.

Climb down out of that tower you've built around yourself, and build a bridge to others across that moat.

There's a whole big world out there waiting for you.

LIVING IN HIS REFLECTION

For now we see in a mirror, dimly, but then face to face....
then I shall know just as I also am known.

—1 Corinthians 13:12

*I*f I could change anything that has happened in my life, I would change the amount of precious time I spent pursuing dreams and using my gifts in ways that God did not bless. How many times have we all said, "I wish I had known then what I know now"?

I've learned not everything that looks like a good opportunity actually is. I've also learned God doesn't always intend for me to walk through a door just because it is open, and the more successful I become sometimes the harder it is to tell the difference between what God is telling me to do and what I'm convincing myself is God's will. It really is true that the way to eternal life is narrow and the path is steep. The same is true of a blessed life on earth. The most wonderful thing is, no matter how many wrong turns I made going up that steep road, God always led me back to himself. You are going to have to be smart, wise, and discerning if you are going to shatter your illusions about love and marriage and break through the glass that's keeping you from seeing the face of God. It won't be easy or a whole lot of fun, but you will experience unspeakable joy when you finally do.

NOT EVERYTHING THAT LOOKS LIKE A GOOD OPPORTUNITY ACTUALLY IS.

DOORS GOD DIDN'T OPEN

Last year I took a job as an instructor at a well-known and prestigious university in North Carolina, teaching social workers. The job required me to travel all over the state, working as many as sixty hours a week and living away from home two or three nights just about every week. Not only that, when I wasn't traveling to training centers, the commute to my office on campus was a grueling 110 miles round trip through heavy Research Triangle traffic. But I convinced myself that I could do it.

I knew when I took the job that I wouldn't have time to do the therapy or the writing that I had always believed was God's call on my life. But at the time I reasoned that since my writing career had not really become that successful yet, and therapy was not as high-paying as teaching, I would probably do better to take the university position.

How like Satan to offer the most delicious-looking apple just when I was on the verge of walking into my calling as a Christian writer. How like me to convince myself that I hadn't heard God tell me otherwise.

I knew the university was very liberal and anti-Christian and that many of the people I'd be working with would have beliefs different from mine. But I squelched those concerns and decided I could just blend in with the crowd. That was a huge mistake. When a person seeks to follow Christ, she cannot blend in with the crowd.

I felt uneasy when I signed the contract, but I pushed my niggling doubts away, justifying my actions by convincing myself that God would never have opened such an enticing door if he had not wanted me to walk through it. Never mind that I'd heard a "still, small voice" whisper otherwise. Never mind that I was forsaking the career I'd been training for most of my life. The fruit at the top of that tree was just too sweet. I bit the apple. And it was one of the most disappointing experiences of my life.

However, even when we disobey God and make mistakes, he uses them to teach us. Nothing is ever wasted in God's economy. My experience taught me a big lesson in obedience, discernment, and spiritual warfare. Deep down I knew I was being disobedient by taking that job. I knew I had other choices. I took the job because I wanted the prestige of being on the faculty of a major university, whether it pleased God or not.

It didn't take me long to figure out I was in the wrong place, though I struggled to keep my job. The final straw came when I realized that some of the curriculum I was going to have to teach violated biblical principles. Still, I fought to hold on, more from pride than anything else. No matter how hard I tried to keep a low profile, whenever someone started in on secular humanist jargon, my spirit would rise up. I had to make it clear where I stood with Christ. That was especially dangerous in an election year. I might as well have been a mouse in a roomful of hungry cats!

Finally, I gave up and resigned. The very day after, I received a call from the publisher about this book proposal. I built my private practice while I wrote the book. It has been a perfect career for me.

God knew all along what he was doing.

I suppose you might be shocked that someone my age, who has been walking with the Lord as long as I have, can still blatantly disobey from time to time. But it is the truth. I am telling you because I don't want you to think that I'm on some kind of spiritual pedestal pointing a well-manicured finger at you. I will be the first to admit I am still a work in progress.

Awhile back, I was reading one of Max Lucado's books in which he admitted that one recent day he found himself in a convenience store buying a beer, even though he'd vowed to give up liquor many years before.

THE DEEPER OUR WALK WITH HIM, THE MORE GOD EXPECTS US TO DEPEND ON THAT VOICE, NOT OUR OWN VAIN THOUGHTS AND IMAGINATIONS.

I admire him immensely, but since reading that confession I admire him even more. We need to be honest about our failures and our temptations. How else can we encourage others who think that they cannot overcome addictions, whether they are to romance, beer, or career egotism?

LIVING IN HIS REFLECTION

If you are going to break out of your old ways of thinking and quit yearning for something you don't have, you have to realize that life is full of choices. Some will be big, some will be small, but unless you really listen to God and obey him, you are going to fall right back into your old negative patterns.

Jesus said, "My sheep listen to my voice" (John 10:27 NIV). The deeper our walk with him, the more he expects us to depend on that voice, not our own vain thoughts and imaginations. He might shut a door for a new Christian, but he will expect a seasoned Christian to be able to choose from many open doors.

God can change you if you let him. But living in his reflection requires that you know him intimately, and that won't happen unless you seek him daily. It won't happen unless you read his Word as often as possible too.

I connect to God while walking on a country path and praying, or when I'm sitting on my old wooden swing, or as I'm driving along a quiet rural road. Sometimes my best talks with God come while I'm cooking a meal or listening to peaceful music.

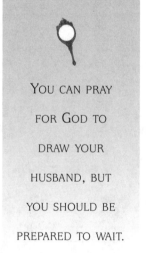

YOU CAN PRAY FOR GOD TO DRAW YOUR HUSBAND, BUT YOU SHOULD BE PREPARED TO WAIT.

I don't say a lot these days when I am with God. I have to talk a lot in my work, and by the time I get to God I'm really kind of talked out. I just like to sit and think about him and feel his love flowing through me like warm honey when I'm tired and my muscles ache. I just like being with him.

I think a lot about whether or not I lived up to what he wanted for me that day, or I simply ask him to help me live out his will during the day to come. I focus on listening for his voice and lifting up the needs of others I know who've asked for prayer. I ask him to protect my family and loved ones. I pray about the things that are bothering me.

But mostly I just thank him for being such a good Father, because I know that he loves me and will do what is needed in my life.

I trust him.

It's taken me years to get to this point. And I've more growing to do. We are all on a journey to draw closer to the Lord. It takes some of us longer than others. He knows where you are on that path, and he is waiting patiently for you.

But if you're married, what about your husband? What if he isn't at the same place as you are spiritually? That can be difficult, especially when you are told that your husband is supposed to be the spiritual head of the house, but you see that he is not very spiritual at all.

PRAYING FOR YOUR HUSBAND

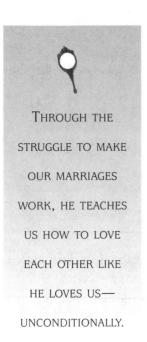

THROUGH THE STRUGGLE TO MAKE OUR MARRIAGES WORK, HE TEACHES US HOW TO LOVE EACH OTHER LIKE HE LOVES US— UNCONDITIONALLY.

God can change your husband, but only if your husband wants to be changed. God won't override the will of another individual. You can pray for God to draw your husband, but you should be prepared to wait. It can take years for that to happen. Sometimes God changes a person by allowing him to walk through many years of pain before the message is received. God rarely just zaps someone on the noggin so that he wakes up one morning mysteriously changed. That is magical thinking at its worst.

When I was a pudgy little kid, I'd dream each night I would wake up thin and svelte in the morning. I was a child then and didn't know any better. Now I realize that a lot of sacrifice and self-denial goes into accomplishing my desired weight goals. The same thing is true of praying for someone else's change of heart.

If you are sitting in church Sunday after Sunday, waiting for your husband to go up to the altar and be transformed into the kind of husband you want, then I'm afraid you are going to have a long wait. It is not that men aren't brought into salvation that way—but salvation and sanctification are not the same. Salvation is the only thing a lot of people seem to think they need.

The salvation experience doesn't usually change a person right away, and when it does, the changes aren't so drastic that you feel like you are finally married to that prince. The road to holiness is a steep and winding path, and sometimes it takes a long time for us human beings to get the simplest truths. You have to admit to the need to change first, and pride keeps many men and women from doing that. We suffer a lot because of pride.

But suffering makes us holy.

A Marriage Made in Heaven

It is ironic that when we use the term "a marriage made in heaven," we are most often referring to an easy marriage, inferring that when two perfectly compatible people meet and marry and live happily ever after God is doing it all.

Does this mean that all of us who are in marriages that require a lot of work somehow are married to the wrong people?

No. In fact, I think difficult marriages are "made in heaven" more than we realize. John and Paula Sandford, authors of *The Transformation of the Inner Man* (Victory House, 1982)—is one

AS LONG AS WE ARE OBSESSED WITH OUR OWN HEARTS, GOD CANNOT FULLY ENTER IN.

of my favorite books of all time argue that God actually uses incompatibility with our mates as one of his primary sculpting tools. He uses our differences to provide the tension and friction that grinds the rough edges off our hard hearts and softens them so we can love our fellow human beings with a God kind of love.

I know my husband and I were meant to be together even though I've shared with you how much we struggled through the years to keep our marriage intact. There are just too many things we've both learned about ourselves and about God for it not to have been ordained. I definitely felt on my wedding day that it was God's will for us to marry, even though I was seriously frightened and had a bad case of cold feet.

Frankly, I wasn't sure that I was old enough or mature enough to be married. And though we came close to divorce, I've never really doubted that Rick and I were meant to marry. I do admit I've been angry at both God and my husband on more than one occasion. I was angry because I never expected life—especially marriage—to be so hard.

But I've learned that if people have an easy marriage, it is because they are saints already, they aren't working very hard at becoming Christlike, or God is going to test them in ways other than their marriages. It is not easy marriages that force us to turn to God. If we allow it, it is a difficult marriage that forces us to lean on God. It is then that he transforms us so we can finally see him face-to-face. Through the struggle to make our marriages work, he teaches us how to love each other like he loves us—unconditionally.

KNOWING GOD

I chose the verses at the beginning of this chapter not only because of their reference to a mirror, the metaphor I've used throughout this book, but because of all the verses in the Bible, I think they describe the goals of our lives here on earth the most succinctly.

> WE REALLY ACT AS IF OUR DELIGHT IN THE LORD IS CONTINGENT UPON OUR GETTING THE DESIRES OF OUR HEARTS.

Don't we all just want to "know and be known"? Don't we all just want to be understood and loved for who we are? Isn't that the essence of romance as well?

We want intimacy and understanding. We want someone who knows our thoughts and anticipates our needs. Someone who knows us so well he can look us in the eyes and read our minds.

We want someone to love us so much he would die for us.

But those of us who have romanticized the life journey have become entranced with our own images. As a result, we are not seeing clearly. Like that "in a mirror, dimly" business, our view is blurred. We stare at our own reflections instead of looking for God. We are so obsessed with our own hearts, we can't see into the heart of the Beloved. And as long as we are obsessed with our own hearts, God cannot fully enter in. God cannot fill us with his love.

And we can never fully experience the joy of knowing him.

THE DESIRES OF OUR HEARTS

In my opinion, one of the most misquoted verses in the Bible is Psalm 37:4: "Delight yourself also in the LORD, and He shall give you the desires of your heart."

I've heard women say this over and over, but always in reference to something they wanted on earth, such as a baby, a husband, a better job, or a larger ministry.

The problem is that most of us get it backward. We really act as if our delight in the Lord is contingent upon our getting the desires of our hearts. Our delight is always conditional, or we delight for just a little while and then discouragement sets in.

Delighting is a hard thing for us humans to do. Webster's *New Thesaurus of the English Language* defines the word *delight (in)* as to: "enjoy, like, savor, and luxuriate in." But how many of us luxuriate in and savor our relationship with God when our prayers aren't being answered—when the job is boring and low-paying, when the boss is mean to us, or when the man we married is crude and thoughtless and snores like a freight train? We must learn to delight regardless of our circumstances, our loneliness, our losses, or our discouragements.

James, the half brother of Jesus, said these words: "My brethren, count it all joy when you fall into various trials, knowing that the testing of your faith produces patience" (James 1:2–3).

Delighting in the Lord and "counting it all joy" are much the same thing.

We are not delighting if we are grumbling about our circumstances. The two just cannot coexist. If you are grumbling about a man you vowed before God to love and cherish, then you aren't delighting in the Lord, and there is a good chance you won't get the desires of your heart.

Of course, I know you are thinking that your husband doesn't delight in the Lord either. Well, I'm sorry, but that is between God and your husband. The only thing God requires is for you to be accountable for yourself.

How Do We Delight in the Lord?

We can move the heart of God and show our delight by

- spending time listening to his voice;
- expressing gratitude for the things we already have instead of complaining and fretting about what we haven't been given;
- talking about him to others with love and respect;
- giving up our addictions and crutches and becoming strong and independent;
- always wanting to get to know him better;
- trusting that God will provide even when our husbands don't;
- laughing and chatting with him about small things as well as big things;
- quickly apologizing when we've done something we know is wrong;
- telling him the truth;
- giving up the things we know hurt him;
- hurting in our hearts when we have said or done things that are ungodly and unloving;
- truly believing he loves us, even when he doesn't give us what we want.

Now, read the list again. Do you realize that these are the very same things that will delight your husband and inspire him to change into the kind of man God wants him to be?

You have to find the courage to look your real prince in the face. Focus on the Lord. Give him your desires and your heart, and allow him to transform you into his image.

Then take a hammer to that Magic Mirror.

SINGING IN THE STORM

About fifteen years ago, Rick and I struggled financially. The only thing we owned was a Honda with ninety thousand miles on it, our furniture, and an old pickup truck. We badly wanted a house of our own once again but didn't know how in the world we could afford it. As I recounted in the beginning of this book, we sold our house and business in the recession of the 1980s.

We lived on the coast of North Carolina, worked long hours in low-paying jobs, and were raising two teenagers. One evening after supper I went to my prayer spot in the yard of our rental house and laid my heart out to the Lord.

I told him that if he wanted me to minister to the people of that area, I'd appreciate it if he would provide a house for us to buy that we could call our own. I told him we had no money, but that since he owned the "cattle on a thousand hills" (Ps. 50:10), I knew he could afford it. I told him I would trust him to provide what we could not get on our own, and I asked for patience and understanding if he chose not to give it to us.

Three weeks later, we owned a house. It is a strange story and a bit of a miracle. I cannot tell you the whole story, but to give you an idea of how God worked in this I'll tell you a little piece of it.

The house was an old beach house built right after World War II that had gone into government foreclosure. It sat a couple of blocks from the Bogue Sound, just a few blocks from the Atlantic Beach Causeway. We knew with that location, the house would be a good investment.

It was a sturdy classic Cape Cod, but needed lots of cosmetic work after years of neglect. Since my husband was handy with a hammer and I was pretty good with paint and wallpaper, we figured we could whip it into shape fairly easily. We decided to bid on it without much hope we would win, as we knew there were going to be lots of bidders, some with much better financial situations than ours.

The night before we were to meet with the realtor to finalize our bid, I had a dream. I dreamed about an old man I'd not seen or even thought about in over fifteen years. Now deceased, he'd been a former neighbor in a small town where we had once lived. His name was John McGwiggin, but my children fondly called him "John Jiggins." He rode a bicycle all over town and was the self-proclaimed town historian. He was quite the odd, charming character. The dream was vivid, and at the time, very puzzling. I remember waking up the morning after thinking, "Where did *that* come from?" But I went about my day and dismissed the dream as an odd quirk of memory.

But later that day, I was to learn that it was not just a random event. As I was talking with the realtor about the data I'd faxed her the day before, she glanced at it and noticed that we'd listed accounts in Enfield, the same town where Mr. McGwiggin rode his bicycle. She asked if we'd once lived there. It was an obscure little town several hours' distance away, so I thought her question quite odd. I told her that we had—for about fifteen years. Then to my shock, the next question she asked me was had I known John McGwiggin!

It turns out that he was her dear old uncle and she had visited him often. I witnessed to the young woman about the dream and how I'd prayed about owning a home just a few weeks before. She agreed with me that God was affirming that this was his provision for our lives.

Sure enough, we won the bid on the house over scads of other contenders, and had—down almost to the penny—what we needed to pay closing costs. Within three weeks of my prayer, we owned the house.

We still own that house, and I'm blessed to say I'm using part of the money from this book to turn it into the Sea Dove Christian Retreat Center. I am also blessed to say that house has tripled in value in the last twelve years and will help secure our retirement in the future. The Lord has restored everything we lost and more.

How wonderful it would feel just to be able to drop all the heavy weight of romantic thinking, unfulfilled yearnings, and constant material acquisition.

Two live oak trees grow in the backyard; one of them is probably at least 150 years old. They are massive, full, and beautiful. But the oldest is my favorite because of its incredible size and sheltering presence. I love that tree. It towers three stories above the house and dominates the courtyard over which it presides. I often sit on my back porch swing contemplating that tree and the years that have come and gone since it first sprouted from the ground. It's hard to fathom such a huge tree growing from a tiny seedling.

I imagine that when that tree sprouted, there was no city—no sidewalks, no busy streets, no tourists rushing over the bridge toward the beach.

These days the cars are full of young women or families in a hurry to get to the beach so they can roast in the sun. But back when the tree was just a shrub, the busy street would have been just a dirt road, traversed by an occasional wagon pulled by a horse swishing flies off its hind quarters with its tail. The only sounds other than the creak of the wagon wheels would have been the moan of the wind and the gentle slap of waves against the white sand or maybe the sound of a sea bell clanging in the distance or the cawing sound of gulls. There would have been a panoramic view of the water shining in the distance and maybe a few island ponies grazing on tough marsh grass.

It brings me peace just to think about it.

But every few years a hurricane barrels through that area. No doubt you have seen how ferocious hurricanes are and the damage they bring. Who knows how many hurricanes have come through in a span of 150 years?

In years past, we were smart and evacuated during hurricanes. But on one occasion, the storm was only a Category Two—one of the lesser storms of the season—so we decided to ride it out.

As the storm passed over, the wind lashed, flinging limbs against the windows and causing some smaller cedar trees to split totally down the middle. I worried about my big trees. I couldn't wait for the eye of the storm to pass over so I could assess the damage.

Imagine my amazement when I walked out into the yard and discovered that both trees had dropped just about all of their leaves during the storm—but were still standing! The ground was covered with almost a foot of green leaves, as if it were fall instead of summer.

Live oaks do that during bad storms. I discovered later that live oaks survive to be old trees precisely because they are designed to drop all their leaves during high winds. They divest themselves of the foliage that weighs them down. They drop their leaves so their limbs don't break when they are tossed by high winds. If they didn't, they would be so damaged they might die.

Wouldn't it be wonderful if we knew how to do that naturally as well—if we could quit worrying about how we look and whether we're beautiful, smart, and have accomplished enough? How wonderful it would feel just to be able to drop all the heavy weight of romantic thinking, unfulfilled yearnings, and constant material acquisition. If we could be like that tree …

But that was not the only miracle that day. While I stood on that porch, I noticed a tiny bird sitting on one of the highest branches, singing its little heart out, right in the middle of a hurricane. I couldn't believe my eyes or my ears! That little bird knew how to take delight, and it wasn't a bit worried about whether or not it measured up to all the other creatures in God's kingdom. It didn't care if it was smart, well feathered, or as pretty as the other little birds. It never questioned its Original Design or looked into a Mirror.

And it sang one of the most beautiful songs I've ever heard.

ORIGINAL DESIGN
INVENTORY

The following is not a test and there are no right or wrong answers. There is no cumulative score that will categorize you in any manner or give you a profile that defines you. It is up to you to decide your Original Design. This is only a series of questions that will help point you toward an idea of how God may have designed you and what he may have planned for your life before your mind was molded by worldly thinking and false messages. You do not have to change everything about yourself (career, lifestyle, etc.) in order to line yourself back up with your Original Design, but this inventory may help you understand why many things about your life may not be bringing you the joy you could be experiencing. God is working in the midst of your life regardless of how far you have strayed from his original purposes.

The basic premise is that we can have a clearer picture of what God may have intended for our lives by looking back at the age when we were the most carefree, innocent, and pure but able to reason and solve problems. For most people, that is somewhere between the ages of seven and twelve.

If you were abused or going through stressful circumstances most of your childhood, I would suggest you take the inventory, but with the realization that you may have difficulty remembering good things. You might have to work hard at imagining what your happy child would have been like had you not been abused.

I suggest you keep an Original Design journal to record your answers to these questions and to save thoughts and reflections as you take this journey through time. Try to envision yourself as accurately as possible and to imagine what this child would say if you met her today. Savor this process and do not push yourself to remember.

Some find it helpful to write a paragraph describing themselves and to place a picture of themselves at that age in front of them as they answer these questions. You may want to paste this picture in your journal.

1. When did you first begin to experience the presence of God in your life?
2. How did that make you feel? Did anything special happen?
3. What is the age prior to puberty that you remember being the most happy?
4. What, at that age, made you happy? Be as specific as possible.
5. Name three things you did as a child that you loved but that you don't do now.
6. What is your birth order?
7. Which parent are you most like? Which parent do you most admire?
8. Which sibling did you relate to the most and what is that person like now?

9. Name the person in your life outside of your immediate family who influenced you the most. Describe that person. Did you admire him or her? If so, why?

10. When did you first start thinking about what you wanted to be when you grew up? Describe what that was.

11. Do you remember being told you shouldn't try what you most wanted to do when you grew up because you wouldn't be good at it, it would be too hard, or there wouldn't be enough money? Did it change your thinking?

12. Do you remember anyone ever telling you what you *should* do when you grew up because they felt they understood you? What did they say?

13. Prior to puberty do you remember your parents praising you for things you didn't particularly enjoy doing because they thought you'd be successful at them?

14. Describe yourself as a teenager. Were you happy?

15. When do you first remember feeling that the world was a scary place and you might not fit in? When do you think your happy child decided to hide?

16. Was there a specific incident that caused you to lose confidence in yourself?

17. When did you first start seeing yourself as an unhappy child?

18. Most women have an internalized image of what a "perfect woman" should look like (socially, emotionally, physically, spiritually, etc.). Describe her.

19. List the ways you fall short of that picture of the perfect woman.

20. What would you need to do to say good-bye to the perfect woman who is keeping your happy child from coming out of hiding?

21. If your happy child were to emerge, how would that change who you are now?

22. If you could close your eyes and picture yourself as a happy, contented person now, what would that look like?

23. What do you need to do to say good-bye to your unhappy child?

24. List three things you are going to start doing in your life now that will allow your happy child to resurface.

25. Write a paragraph that sums up your Original Design and how your life must change now so you can start being the person God intended for you to be all along. Begin telling your unhappy child that you don't need her anymore. Invite your happy child (the real you) to come out of hiding.

EXPLANATIONS OF QUESTIONS:

Questions 1–5: These questions will help clarify when God first began to interact with you as a person. For some this is very early, but others have no recollection of sensing the presence of God, or they were in too much stress/conflict to experience God. We need to understand how this affected our view of ourselves.

Prior to puberty, our childhood aspirations and favorite pastimes contain seeds of a vision for what God could do in our lives.

Questions 6–13: Birth order will tell you a great deal about yourself and how you view your role in the world. You may be helped by reading some books on birth order, as it determines our life choices more than we realize.

We inherit basic traits from one parent or the other but sometimes reject those attributes because we don't like that parent. Unfortunately, we tend to model ourselves after the parent we consider dominant even if that parent is not following God's will. We end up not liking ourselves very much, but we don't know how to change.

We're often unaware of the ways in which our role models influenced us. It's important to know if your role model was someone God used to mold your mind or someone who caused you to move away from your Original Design. Interactions with siblings or older relatives are especially important, and their opinions can change our lives forever. The same is true for friends.

Questions 14–20: Adolescence is when rebellion, confusion, and physical urges begin to redirect and sabotage your Original Design. Until you isolate these aspects of yourself that are not authentic to your nature (the unhappy child and the perfect woman) and begin to break their rule over your life, your Original Design will remain hidden. Pray a specific prayer asking God to help you say good-bye to these aspects of yourself.

Questions 21–25: Get to know your happy child and invite her to return!

Daily Original Design Prayer

Lord, by you I was fearfully and wonderfully made. You created me with a plan in mind. You created me to be happy and to experience abundant life. Forgive me, Father, if I have strayed from your plan for my life. Help me to

*bring my life back in line with the way you designed me
and planned for me to live. Please reveal what is missing
from my life that I used to enjoy and what I need to change
to get back to your Original Design for me. Give me the
courage to say good-bye to those aspects of myself that are
keeping me bound in unhappiness and false beliefs. Help me
to find my happy child once again so that I can worship
and enjoy our relationship as you truly intended. Amen.*

Resource List

Books

Beattie, Melody. *Codependent No More*. Center City, MN: Hazelton Foundation, 1986.

Cloninger, Claire and Karla Worley. *When the Shoe Doesn't Fit*. Birmingham, AL: New Hope Publishers, 2003.

Eldredge, John and Brent Curtis. *The Sacred Romance*. Nashville: Nelson, 1997.

Everson, Eva Marie and Jessica Everson. *Sex, Lies, and the Media*. Colorado Springs: Cook Communications, 2005.

Frost, Jack. *Embracing the Father's Love*. Conway, SC: Father's House Productions, 2002.

Goleman, Daniel. *Emotional Intelligence*. New York: Bantam, 1995.

Hendrix, Harville. *Getting the Love You Want*. New York: Owl Books, 2001.

———. *Receiving Love*. New York: Atria, 2005.

Johnson, Toni Cavanagh. *Understanding Your Child's Sexual Behavior: What's Natural and Healthy*. South Pasadena, CA: New Harbinger Publications, 1999.

Love, Pat. *The Truth About Love.* New York: Fireside, 2001.

Meyer, Joyce. *Approval Addiction.* New York: Joyce Meyer Trade, 2005.

Norwood, Robin. *Women Who Love Too Much.* New York: Simon and Schuster, 1995.

Russianoff, Penelope. *When Am I Going to be Happy?* New York: Bantam, 1986.

Sandford, John and Paula Sandford. *Healing the Wounded Spirit.* Tulsa, OK: Victory House, 1985.

————. *Transformation of the Inner Man.* Tulsa, OK: Victory House, 1982.

Smalley, Gary. *The DNA of Relationships.* Wheaton, IL: Tyndale House Publishers, 2004.

Stone, Charles and Heather Stone. *Daughters Gone Wild, Dads Gone Crazy.* Nashville: W Publishing Group, 2003.

Tabb, Mark. *Mission to Oz.* Chicago: Moody Press, 2004.

Wright, H. Norman. *Always Daddy's Girl.* Ventura, CA: Regal Books, 2001.

————. *Communication: Key to Marriage.* Ventura, CA: Regal Books, 2000.

————. *A Dad Shaped Hole in My Heart.* Minneapolis: Bethany House Publishers, 2005.

WEB SITES

www.aacc.net (American Association of Christian Counselors)

www.barna.org

www.mentalhealth.org

www.ndvh.org (National Domestic Violence Hotline: 1-800-799-SAFE)

www.protectkids.com

Check www.deborahdunn.com for links to more Web sites.

READERS' GUIDE

for Personal Reflection or
Group Discussion

READERS' GUIDE

*S*ince childhood, many of us have received false, romantic viewpoints of what life is supposed to be like. Our culture's romanticized emphasis on marriage and preoccupation with outward beauty, for example, have given us distorted perspectives concerning ourselves, God, and others. We have tried to live according to the Magic Mirror—and it hasn't worked well.

Slammed by the realities of challenging marriages, imperfect families, self-esteem issues, and make-believe expectations of how life should treat us, we struggle to find purpose and meaning. We remain unhappy no matter what we achieve in life and how many things we possess.

The idealized vision of the perfect life turns out to be a shaky foundation on which to build. The lives we dreamed of haven't reconciled with real life. We so easily pretend that painful things never happened and constantly crave affirmation and approval. We even find ourselves denying our feelings of failure and unhappiness and working harder just to keep things from crumbling.

We realize we won't become Cinderellas and that our so-called princes may never meet our expectations, so we drift and sometimes seek short-term pleasure in destructive relationships and addictions. Often we compete so hard to be better than other women that we sacrifice friendships with them. We do things not because we truly enjoy them, but because they elicit attention and praise.

The following questions are designed to aid and encourage you, and perhaps other women in a small group, to reflect on important topics. Discover how to develop significant relationships with godly women. Explore how to stop living out the expectations other people had for your life and find peace and self-worth in God.

Enjoy this opportunity to discover who you really are, the purposes God has designed for you to fulfill, and the life that will bring you joy and peace—and overflow to other people.

Set aside time to think about these questions, to face issues that surface. Ask God to help you experience the joy, growth, and strength he offers. With his help, you'll break out of the Magic Mirror's distortions and delight in seeing yourself, God, and other people through God's true and loving reflection.

CHAPTER ONE

1. When you were young, what did you believe about marriage and family? What expectations did you develop as a result? In what way(s) were your views similar to or different from the author's views?

2. How has your life differed from a life full of adventure and romance? Why does our culture often emphasize false pictures of what the future will be like?

3. What, as you were growing up, did people teach you was your real purpose in life?

4. In what way(s) have you struggled to reconcile your real life with the life you've always dreamed of having? How has this struggle affected you?

5. What do women you know do to make up for the deep voids they have inside? (Eating junk food? Reading romance novels?) What tools do you use to try to cope? (Be honest!)

6. What ingredients do you think will create a magical and happy life?

CHAPTER TWO

1. How do you typically respond when your spouse doesn't even come close to meeting your expectations?

2. To what extent do you find yourself trying to please people rather than God? Why is this distinction important to recognize?

3. How do you measure your self-worth?

4. Many women believe that if they are just good enough, pray more, and work harder at being a perfect wife that everything will change—especially their husbands. What is wrong with this belief? Why?

5. When we view our husbands as princes, what kind of pressure does that put on us? On them?

CHAPTER THREE

1. In what way(s) has secular television programming encouraged us to form irrational and false beliefs about life?

2. Do you agree that women today are in more bondage to romantic thinking than they were years ago? Why or why not?

3. As you were growing up, how did your family and friends view the romantic content of secular television programs?

4. How might a woman's dissatisfaction with her husband relate to her dissatisfaction with herself?

5. Are there ways your husband shows you real, biblical love even when he isn't demonstrating romantic love? How are you showing him real love?

6. What types of things do women do to fill the empty space created by anxiety about their husbands' waning attention and the loss of the romantic experience?

CHAPTER FOUR

1. What is a "Big Event"? What Big Events have occurred in your life?

2. List some of the Big Events that are now taking place even in the lives of children. How can we know which of these are fun and healthy—and which may be teaching children the wrong messages?

3. In what way(s) does living for the next Big Event affect one's ability to face a lack of true richness and meaning?

4. Why can't Big Events make us happy?

5. When you need to do important internal work, what kinds of external events do you use to distract yourself from that process?

6. To what extent have you received the full, satisfying, and abundant life Christ has for you?

7. The author shares why she began shopping in thrift stores. What changes might you make in order to maximize your time and effort in furthering the kingdom of God?

CHAPTER FIVE

1. What is your first memory of being ashamed of yourself? How did you deal with the shame?

2. In which area(s) has sin entered your life and possibly taken root? Why is it that the more of that "apple" we eat, the more we seem to crave?

3. Like the queen in the story of *Snow White and the Seven Dwarfs*, many women today gain self-worth from their reflections in the Mirror. How has the Mirror influenced your view of yourself?

4. What kinds of things do we do in order to stand out above other people?

5. Do you agree with the author that many women will always be dissatisfied with themselves—no matter what they achieve in life—until they commit their lives to Christ and are discipled by a mature Christian? Why or why not?

6. What types of things do women do in order to receive validation from the Magic Mirror?

CHAPTER SIX

1. How have you, or others you know, been wounded by the church? What steps might you take to create and/or encourage godly community and break patterns of secretive and closed communication?

2. Which problems in the Christian home are you familiar with? What is a "toxic" secret, and how does such deception affect family members?

3. Why can keeping up appearances be so harmful to us?

4. When you feel depressed and lose confidence in your worth, how do you typically respond?

5. Reflect on your past. Which obstacles do you face when you think about confronting your hidden wounds?

6. How might you, and others you know, develop a community in which you can talk honestly and face your Magic Mirror issues together, mutually supporting one another?

Chapter Seven

1. What are some of the things that cause us to feel lost and make it difficult to find our way back to God and forget painful memories?

2. How might churches better deal with people who are in the darkness? Might you be willing to pitch in and try to help struggling women? Why or why not?

3. How does God's voice differ from the voice coming from the Mirror?

4. Why is it often easy to return to sinful things or relation-ships we know are harmful—even when we have made progress in facing them? Why do we keep going back into the dark woods of our sin?

5. How can we address painful things in our pasts and receive healing from them?

6. What tips did the author offer concerning how we can find people to help us face our darkness?

Chapter Eight

1. What is the world's idealized version of what we should be? How is this different from God's view of us?

2. Why is it important to understand our Original Design?

3. What kinds of things would you truly love to do—but for whatever reason have not done them? What steps might you implement in order to start rediscovering things you love?

4. In which particular area(s) have you listened more to the world than to your own quiet voice and the voice of God?

5. Would you really like to become the person God intended you to be? Why or why not? What steps might you take to be in his will and find your right calling?

6. What do you think is the relationship between recapturing your Original Design and living in godly obedience and walking in faith? What does this kind of obedience and faith look like in everyday life?

CHAPTER NINE

1. How does real love toward your spouse differ from romantic love?

2. What have you done to try to get your husband to change in order to please you?

3. Why is it so important for a married couple to make a deliberate effort to communicate effectively? What can they do to keep from misunderstanding each other's motives and intentions?

4. The author stated, "Women cannot change men, only God can change men.... The basis of true love is acceptance." What would happen if you stepped back and allowed God to change your husband?

5. What's involved in embracing the man your husband is instead of the man you want him to be?

6. What are some practical ways in which we can build up and praise our husbands, focusing on the good things about them?

CHAPTER TEN

1. In what way(s) have you, or someone you love, avoided God's real call by staying busy with projects? What happened as a result?

2. Describe what happens when a person tries to get her needs met through family life and church instead of God.

3. How might your life be different if you focused on serving Christ more rather than enabling a lifestyle that feeds your need for affirmation and approval?

4. What does God provide for each of us when we are called to do a particular task? What, if any, provision can we expect from God when we are driven to do things in his name that he never called us to do?

5. How will we view serving others, according to the author, when we form a relationship with God and love him?

6. What role might strong female friends who know God have in helping us move from codependence to healing?

Chapter Eleven

1. Why is it so important for each of us to have girlfriends who walk with God and love us unconditionally? What are the joys of such relationships?

2. What are some definitions of a real girlfriend?

3. Which of the "finding friends" tips resonated with you? Why? How might you start implementing some of these tips this coming week?

4. What are some reasons for finding mentors—women who will come alongside you and provide wisdom and encouragement?

5. If you were to pursue positive activities that provide excitement, adventure, and growth, what would they be? Why? What attitudes or beliefs may be limiting your pursuit of these things?

6. How might you take healthy risks and learn new things that will challenge you to think differently and help you to grow?

Chapter Twelve

1. Why is it important to distinguish between what God is telling you to do and what you are convincing yourself is God's will?

2. Which choices are you thinking about making that will help you break out of your old ways of thinking and quit yearning for something you don't have?

3. In order to live in God's reflection, we each need to know him intimately. What is involved in this process?

4. Do you trust God? Why or why not?

5. Are you ready now to look for God instead of staring at your own reflection? Why or why not? Why can't God fully enter our lives while we are obsessed with our own hearts?

6. Reread Psalm 34:7. What do you think it means to "delight" in the Lord?

Books on the Lighter Side of Family Life
by Rhonda Rhea

Amusing Grace

Amusing Grace is the perfect Rx for every mom! Get ready to laugh until you can't stop as you gain nuggets of wisdom through the everyday escapades of a mom of five!

ISBN: 0-78143-532-3 • Item #: 93823
5-1/2 x 8-1/2 • Paperback • 128P

Turkey Soup for the Soul
Tastes Just Like Chicken!

Rhonda Rhea is the Christian readers' Erma Bombeck! Her uncanny eye for life's details will leave your sides aching, your spirit revived, and your faith renewed!

ISBN: 0-78144-130-7 • Item #: 103634
5-1/2 x 8-1/2 • Paperback • 192P

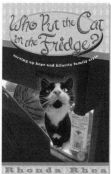

Who Put the Cat in the Fridge?

The Rhea household is living proof that humor is possibly the best—if not the only way to stay sane in the busy world of today's families! Rhonda takes a hilarious look at herself, the joy of being a pastor's wife, and the domestic demands of raising five kids.

ISBN: 0-78144-190-0 • Item #: 103952
5-1/2 x 8-1/2 • Paperback • 256P

The Word at Work Around the World

A vital part of Cook Communications Ministries is our international outreach, Cook Communications Ministries International (CCMI). Your purchase of this book, and of other books and Christian-growth products from Cook, enables CCMI to provide Bibles and Christian literature to people in more than 150 languages in 65 countries.

Cook Communications Ministries is a not-for-profit, self-supporting organization. Revenues from sales of our books, Bible curricula, and other church and home products not only fund our U.S. ministry, but also fund our CCMI ministry around the world. One hundred percent of donations to CCMI go to our international literature programs.

CCMI reaches out internationally in three ways:

· Our premier International Christian Publishing Institute (ICPI) trains leaders from nationally led publishing houses around the world.

· We provide literature for pastors, evangelists, and Christian workers in their national language.

· We reach people at risk—refugees, AIDS victims, street children, and famine victims—with God's Word.

Word Power, God's Power

Faith Kidz, RiverOak, Honor, Life Journey, Victor, NexGen — every time you purchase a book produced by Cook Communications Ministries, you not only meet a vital personal need in your life or in the life of someone you love, but you're also a part of ministering to José in Colombia, Humberto in Chile, Gousa in India, or Lidiane in Brazil. You help make it possible for a pastor in China, a child in Peru, or a mother in West Africa to enjoy a life-changing book. And because you helped, children and adults around the world are learning God's Word and walking in his ways.

Thank you for your partnership in helping to disciple the world. May God bless you with the power of his Word in your life.

For more information about our international ministries, visit www.ccmi.org.

Additional copies of *Trapped in the Magic Mirror*
are available wherever good books are sold.

If you have enjoyed this book,
or if it has had an impact on your life,
we would like to hear from you.

Please contact us at:

LIFE JOURNEY
Cook Communications Ministries, Dept. 201
4050 Lee Vance View
Colorado Springs, CO 80918

Or at our Web site: www.cookministries.com

LIFE JOURNEY®
Bringing Home the Message for Life